MW00563890

GOOD HOUSEKEEPING
Air Fryer Magic

**Pepperoni
Pizza**

page 93

GOOD HOUSEKEEPING

Air Fryer Magic

75 Easy Recipes for Frying, Roasting & Baking

HEARST
HOME

23

41

103

147

contents

Tandoori-Style Chicken

page 71

Introduction

Counter space is a hot commodity in almost every kitchen, but millions of people (us included!) can agree that an air fryer is one hundred percent worth making room for. In the decade following the launch of the first air fryer from Philips, we have witnessed this countertop appliance go from a trendy wild-card buy to a mainstream must-purchase item. Air fryer sales have skyrocketed over the past few years, with more than 25 million units making their way into American homes.

At Good Housekeeping, we have been testing and recommending the best air fryers since the beginning. Like so many other people, we started out by using the air fryer as an alternative to a deep fryer—cooking up favorite foods without as much oil or grease. But as we continued to experiment over the years, we discovered just how versatile and amazing this appliance is. It comes in handy for getting tasty food (from breakfast to dessert!) on the table in almost no time. In these pages, you'll find examples of its magic, with more than 75 recipes made in the air fryer—all developed, tested and tested again (and again!) by the Good Housekeeping Test Kitchen team. Despite its name, it can do much more than crisp up wings and fries.

Kate

KATE MERKER
Chief Food Director

> "It's a game changer when it comes to incorporating vegetables into every meal. I was super impressed with the way you can get results similar to sautéing with way less oil."
>
> **KRISTINA KUREK**
> Recipe Developer

Getting Started

The air fryer achieved MVP status after
turning out thousands of chicken wings and
frozen fries "fried" to crisp perfection,
but its place as a culinary staple was cemented
once everyone learned that this appliance
could do so much more.

TEST KITCHEN TIP

Food placed on a perforated tray or insert, usually inside an air fryer basket, promotes even more air circulation so heat can come into direct contact with food and crisp it up.

Chicken Parm

page 75

Air Fryer 101

With the turn of a dial or the press of a button, an air fryer can cook perfectly browned meats and caramelized veggies — not to mention crunchy snacks and small-batch desserts — in virtually no time. For the best (read: tastiest) results, take some time to familiarize yourself with the machine.

How It Works

First things first: An air fryer is similar to an oven. It can bake and roast, but while conventional ovens usually have heat sources at the bottom (sometimes with a secondary source at the top), the heating elements in an air fryer are typically located only at the top of the appliance and are accompanied by a large, powerful fan. This combination of concentrated heat and a fan that circulates the hot air (along with an air fryer's compact size) results in super-crispy, evenly cooked food with little to no oil needed. Plus, an air fryer requires barely any preheating time, so you can cook foods in it even faster than in a conventional oven.

Cooking chicken breasts in the air fryer — and discovering how juicy and delicious they turn out! — completely redefined my relationship with this appliance. Now it's an essential part of my weeknight dinner routine.

TRISH CLASEN MARSANICO
Deputy Food Editor

Types of Air Fryers

When shopping for an air fryer, it's important to consider how many people you're typically cooking for. A smaller air fryer (1.2 liters) is good for one or two people, while a medium-size appliance (3 to 4 liters) can serve two or three and the largest ones (6 or more liters) are best for families of four to six.

There are tons of variations in size, style and power, but you'll most commonly find these two types of air fryers.

TOASTER-OVEN-STYLE

If countertop space is a concern, this multitasking air-fryer style earns its spot. In addition to air-frying, these models can toast, bake, broil and more (some have dehydrating and pizza-making functions as well).

BASKET-STYLE

These models are great for large batches of foods like fries and vegetables that benefit from shaking to toss them (more on this on page 14!), and they are usually easy to clean because the basket can be placed directly in the dishwasher. Also, you don't have to worry as much about oils dripping onto an exposed heat source and burning (as can happen with some toaster-oven models).

Tried + Tested Air Fryers

In the Good Housekeeping Institute's Kitchen Appliances and Innovation Lab, the team spends a lot of time air-frying! They have cooked 50 pounds of wings and hundreds of homemade fries and torn open dozens of bags of frozen foods while testing more than 40 air fryers to find the best ones.

BEST OVERALL

Ninja Air Fryer Max XL

The Fryer Max was the top performer in our air fryer tests. It scored the highest marks across the board for ease of use thanks to its intuitive, easy-to-read buttons and clear owner's manual. During our tests, the air fryer basket slid in and out easily, which made handling a breeze. We're fans of the basket's removable tray and its slick ceramic-coated interior, which makes it nonstick. The insert fits snugly and securely on the bottom of the basket so you don't have to worry about it falling out when you turn the food out onto a plate. Both are dishwasher-safe and easy to clean, even if you choose to hand-wash.

In addition to being easy to use, the Ninja Air Fryer Max XL scored the highest for performance. It produced crisp and evenly cooked frozen fries, homemade fries and chicken wings that were moist on the inside. The model we tested comes with a broiling rack for even quicker and juicier results, and it offers a fast way to create melty cheese. It also

a note on adjusting recipes

No two air fryers are the same so we highly recommend taking time to get to know your appliance. Experiment! Check in on your food! It's OK to pull the basket out at any time during the cooking cycle, especially if you smell something burning. Most models will automatically shut off while the basket is out or the door is open and resume when the basket is pushed back in or the door is closed. If food isn't cooked when the timer goes off, set a timer for a few extra minutes and continue cooking. As you use your air fryer more, you'll better understand whether it cooks faster, hotter or slower than others and you can adapt each recipe accordingly.

The variety of desserts that can be baked in an air fryer was eye-opening! It's so easy to whip up quality, small-batch treats.

JOY CHO
Assistant Food Editor

features several cook settings, including Max Crisp and Air Broil (which both reach 450°F) and Dehydrate (which reaches a low of 105°F). The various settings are programmed with unique maximum and minimum temperatures so you can select them to achieve different cooking results. Another unique feature is the timer, which counts down in seconds. For a larger capacity, consider the Ninja Foodi 6-in-1 2-Basket Air Fryer. It performs as well as the Air Fryer Max XL with more versatility.

BEST BASKET-STYLE AIR FRYER

Instant Vortex Air Fryer

Air fryers from Instant, the brand that makes Instant Pot multicookers, have been on our list of the best air fryers sincewe started testing them. The models we tested, including this one, are easy to program and high-performing. This one particularly stands out for its large square-shaped basket, which maximizes cooking space, is easy to slide out

and maneuver and fits comfortably in the dishwasher.In our tests, chicken wings came out crispy, golden and juicy and frozen fries were moist but crisp and evenly cooked without being shaken midway through. This air fryer has a built-in preheat function, which takes about3 ½ minutes to reach 400°F and chirps when it's ready to cook.

BEST TOASTER-OVEN-STYLE AIR FRYER

Cuisinart Convection Toaster Oven

Cuisinart was one of the first brands to introduce a toaster oven air fryer that allows you to toast, bake, air-fry and convection bake. We tested this digital version, which made not only the crispiest air-fried food in the shortest time out of all the air fryers we tested but also some of the most evenly colored toast in our toaster oven test. The rectangular 15.5- by 16-inch air-frying rack offers a large cooking surface (especially compared with basket-style air fryers) and sits atop a drip/crumb tray for easy cleanup.

> When my oven broke, I realized it's so easy and versatile. It can help with meal prep or create a healthy dinner and even a dessert. There's no need to turn on your oven during an NYC summer when you have an air fryer!

TINA MARTINEZ
Food Producer

> Everyone is always shocked to hear how quickly salmon cooks in the air fryer, with barely any additional ingredients. I usually add just oil and salt — that's it!

NICOLE PAPANTONIOU
Kitchen Appliances and Innovation Lab Director

Scan for more expert air fryer reviews!

Set Yourself Up for Success

In the Good Housekeeping Test Kitchen, the team has created and tested nearly 200 recipes in the air fryer. Along the way, we have cooked up 150 pounds of vegetables and more than 80 fish fillets and indulged in dozens of dreamy sweets, learning a lot in the process. Here are some of our most helpful discoveries.

Skip nonstick cooking spray.

Aerosolized cooking sprays often contain processed oils and additives that, while considered safe by the FDA, might not be your best bet. They don't taste great, and the buildup from their use can leave residue on nonstick surfaces and cause food to stick over time. Instead, brush the air-fryer tray or basket with oil or melted butter or use a refillable spray bottle. Some meats don't require any oil, while in other cases you can toss the food with oil instead of coating the basket.

Give everything space.

Overcrowding and overfilling the air fryer runs counter to its core function. When hot air circulates around food, the food gets crispy. If food pieces are too close together and/or stacked in layers, the air will not be able to reach the food, leaving you with sad, soggy steamed results. To ensure the crispiest foods, arrange pieces in a single layer, leaving space between them. This usually means you need to work in batches.

Strategically shake and flip foods.

For smaller ingredients (think fries, vegetables and snack mixes), shaking the basket halfway through cooking helps make sure everything gets evenly cooked. For larger ingredients such as chicken breasts, fish fillets or bacon, use tongs to flip halfway through cooking, unless you're looking for a browned, "seared" effect. In our tests, we found that it was better to allow one side to cook longer to achieve this. (Note: We developed all these recipes with optimal browning in mind.)

Season smartly.

Often when cooking in an air fryer, it makes sense to stick to dry seasonings, herbs and spices — less moisture added to your food leads to crispier results. That said, you can (and should!) try incorporating saucier ingredients into your air-fryer meals. Be careful, though, and wait to baste meats with anything with sugar (think honey or BBQ sauce) until the last couple of minutes of cooking — otherwise you'll risk having everything burn.

a note on timing

Because all air fryers are slightly different, the total times for these recipes will shift based on how hot your air fryer gets as well as the size of your air fryer. If you are working with a smaller air fryer and need to air-fry the food in batches, that will add to the total time. The reverse is also true.

Top Tools

SILICONE- OR NYLON-TIPPED TONGS

Most air fryer models have a basket with nonstick coating, so you do not want to scrape the surface with metal utensils.

REFILLABLE SPRAY BOTTLES

It's best to avoid aerosolized cooking sprays. Add your go-to oil to a refillable bottle and then give the air fryer a little spritz before startingto cook.

INSTANT-READ THERMOMETER

When cooking meat, it's essential to know when it is fully cooked—and there's no better way than by checking its temp.

HEAT-RESISTANT SURFACES

Use caution and always set the basket and accessories on a heat-resistant counter, a silicone pad or a trivet when cooking is complete.

Quick-Fix Donuts

page 155

If your air fryer smells bad while you're cooking or starts to smoke, there is probably baked-on residue on or near the heating element. Time for a deep-clean!

Sourdough- and Gruyère- Stuffed Mushrooms

page 63

Keep It Clean

Good news: You don't need to deal with cooling and discarding a ton of oil as you would with a deep fryer. And many air fryer models have dishwasher-safe parts. So cleanup is a breeze! Follow these easy instructions to keep your air fryer like new.

Basket-Style

1. Turn off and unplug the air fryer and let it cool completely. Pull out the drawer and remove the basket or tray.

2. Dispose of any excess oil and wash the removable parts in warm, soapy water or place any dishwasher-safe parts upside down in the top rack of the dishwasher. Use a soft-bristle bottle brush to scrub off any gunk and get into the vents and nooks and crannies of the tray (to protect the metal or nonstick finish). Rinse well and let dry.

3. Wipe down the bottom interior of the air fryer, as well as the exterior, with a damp cloth or paper towel. Replace the basket once clean and dry.

Toaster-Oven-Style

1. Turn off and unplug the air fryer and let it cool completely.

2. Remove the racks and wash in warm, soapy water, using a dish brush to scrub away grease and food bits, or place any dishwasher-safe parts in the top rack of the dishwasher.

3. Empty any oil from the drip tray, but don't pour it down the sink drain. The tray can often be placed in the dishwasher to clean it. Or hand-wash it by rinsing it well and then drying it.

4. Wipe down the bottom interior of the air fryer, as well as the exterior, with a damp cloth or paper towel. Once the trays are clean, place them inside.

Deep-Clean

1. Turn off and unplug the air fryer and let it cool completely.

2. Remove the basket or racks and clean them.

3. Leave the air fryer upright so any gunk you brush off will fall to the bottom and not get caught in the mesh, the heating element or the fan at the top.

4. Use a clean, dry soft-bristle brush to scrub and release burned-on bits from the mesh covering the heating element, then wipe with a damp cloth. Turn the air fryer upside down to clean the heating element.

5. Make a baking soda paste by mixing $1/2$ cup of baking soda with a few tablespoons of water. Use the baking soda paste and a damp soft cloth to gently scrub away the grime.

6. Rinse the cloth with water, wring it out and wipe away the residue. Flip the air fryer right side up and place the clean basket and trays inside.

chapter one

Breakfast

Fire up your air fryer first thing in the morning and you won't regret it. This appliance will satisfy all your sweet, salty, eggy or cheesy desires, from extra-crispy bacon and hash browns to sticky-good cinnamon rolls.

RECIPES

A bonus: the most amazing smells first thing in the morning.

Cinnamon Rolls

Freshly "baked" buns in under an hour? Yes, please. Thanks to store-bought biscuit dough, you can skip the overnight rise that traditional dough needs. And don't forget the glaze! Sour cream adds tang and balances the sweet topping.

ACTIVE TIME 25 minutes   TOTAL TIME 45 minutes   MAKES 12

½ cup pecans

1 16-ounce can refrigerated biscuit dough

All-purpose flour, for rolling

½ cup packed dark brown sugar

2 teaspoons ground cinnamon

¼ teaspoon ground cardamom

2 tablespoons unsalted butter, melted

Canola oil, for brushing

1 cup confectioners' sugar

3 tablespoons sour cream, plus more as needed

½ teaspoon pure vanilla extract

Kosher salt

1. Heat the air fryer to 325°F. Arrange the pecans in an even layer in the air-fryer basket. Air-fry until toasted, about 5 minutes. Finely chop the toasted pecans.

2. Nestle the biscuits together on a lightly floured surface (4 biscuits long and 2 biscuits wide). In a small bowl, combine the brown sugar, cinnamon and cardamom.

3. Squish the biscuits together so there are no gaps between them and roll the dough into an approximately 12- by 10-inch rectangle, sprinkling the dough with flour as needed to prevent sticking and patching up any gaps as you go. Gently stretch the edges as needed to make a rectangular shape.

4. Brush the dough with the butter and sprinkle the brown sugar mixture on top, leaving a ½-inch border along the long end opposite you, then spread with your hands to evenly coat the dough. Sprinkle the pecans on top. Working from the long end closest to you, tightly roll up the dough into a log and pinch the seams closed. Using a sharp knife, slice the log into 12 pieces (each about 1 inch thick).

5. Brush the basket with oil. Working in batches if needed, arrange the cinnamon rolls in the basket, spacing them apart so they're not touching. Air-fry at 325°F until golden brown, 7 to 9 minutes.

6. Meanwhile, in a medium bowl, whisk together the confectioners' sugar, sour cream, vanilla and a big pinch of salt to make a thick but pourable glaze (if the glaze is too thick, add more sour cream, ½ teaspoon at a time, until you achieve the desired consistency). Drizzle the glaze over the warm cinnamon rolls. Serve immediately. Store any leftovers in an airtight container in the refrigerator for up to 5 days.

—

PER SERVING (1 ROLL) *About 245 calories, 10 g fat (3.5 g saturated fat), 3 g protein, 320 mg sodium, 37 g carbohydrates, 1 g fiber*

TEST KITCHEN TIP
Whisk the cinnamon into the melted butter before mixing with any other ingredients to help prevent the spice from clumping.

French Toast Sticks

There's no need to stand over a hot skillet, but be sure to fully soak the bread in the egg-milk mixture, as French toast can dry out faster in the air fryer. What to do with the extra few minutes? Sit and enjoy your coffee while your brunch "cooks."

ACTIVE TIME 25 minutes   TOTAL TIME 30 minutes   SERVES 4

3 tablespoons butter, melted, plus more for brushing

½ teaspoon ground cinnamon

6 large eggs, beaten

1 cup milk

1 tablespoon pure maple syrup, plus more for serving

1½ teaspoons pure vanilla extract

2 tablespoons Grand Marnier (optional)

Kosher salt

4 1-inch-thick slices brioche, cut into 1-inch sticks

Confectioners' sugar, for topping (optional)

Raspberries, for serving

1. In a large bowl, whisk together the butter and cinnamon, then whisk in the eggs, milk, maple syrup, vanilla, Grand Marnier (if using) and a pinch of salt.

2. Transfer the egg mixture to a large baking dish, add the brioche and let sit 2 minutes. Flip the sticks and let soak until nearly all the liquid is absorbed, 6 to 8 minutes more.

3. Heat the air fryer to 400°F. Brush the air-fryer basket with butter. Add half the soaked brioche sticks and air-fry 4 minutes. Using tongs, flip and air-fry until golden brown, 3 to 4 minutes more.

4. Brush the basket with more butter and repeat with the remaining soaked brioche sticks. Two minutes before the second batch is ready, add the first batch back to the air fryer, placing on top of the second batch, to reheat quickly before serving. Sprinkle with sugar if desired and serve with raspberries and more syrup for dipping.
—

PER SERVING *About 400 calories, 25 g fat (13 g saturated fat), 14 g protein, 465 mg sodium, 29 g carbohydrates, 1 g fiber*

Maple-Glazed Sausage

While you can use your air fryer to heat up frozen breakfast sausages, we recommend making your own from scratch. Start with a package of sweet Italian sausage and doctor it up with fresh herbs and lemon zest for added brightness.

ACTIVE TIME 15 minutes   **TOTAL TIME** 25 minutes   **SERVES** 8

- 1 pound sweet Italian sausage, casings removed
- ¼ cup fresh flat-leaf parsley, chopped
- ¼ cup fresh dill, chopped
- ¼ cup fresh chives, chopped
- 1 tablespoon finely grated lemon zest
- 1 tablespoon pure maple syrup, plus more for serving

1. In a medium bowl, mix the sausage, parsley, dill, chives and lemon zest. Form the mixture into 16 small patties, each about ¼ inch thick.

2. Heat the air fryer to 400°F. Working in batches if needed, arrange the sausage patties in the air-fryer basket, spacing about 1 inch apart, and air-fry 4 minutes. Using tongs, flip and cook until golden brown, 2 minutes more. Transfer to a platter and brush with the maple syrup. Serve with extra syrup.
—

PER SERVING *About 110 calories, 8 g fat (2.5 g saturated fat), 6 g protein, 215 mg sodium, 3 g carbohydrates, 0 g fiber*

Psst: Flip to page 51 for another way to use hard-boiled eggs!

4 large eggs
  Ice water, for cooling
⅓ cup mayonnaise
½ tablespoon fresh lemon juice
½ small clove garlic, finely grated
  Kosher salt and pepper
¼ cup fresh basil, chopped
2 tablespoons fresh chives, chopped
8 slices whole-grain bread
2 cups salad greens or favorite lettuce
1 avocado, sliced
½ seedless cucumber, halved crosswise and thinly sliced lengthwise
1 cup sprouts

1. Heat the air fryer to 275°F. Place the eggs in the air-fryer basket and air-fry 15 minutes. Immediately transfer the eggs to a bowl of ice water to cool for a few minutes, then peel and slice the eggs.

2. Meanwhile, in a small bowl, combine the mayo, lemon juice, garlic and ¼ teaspoon each salt and pepper; fold in the basil and chives.

3. Spread the basil mayo on the bread slices, then create the sandwiches by layering the lettuce, avocado, cucumber, sprouts and eggs.

—

PER SERVING *About 280 calories, 17 g fat (9 g saturated fat), 15 g protein, 470 mg sodium, 15 g carbohydrates, 1 g fiber*

Green Goddess Sandwiches

Our Test Kitchen team tried almost every way of cooking an egg, only to confirm that it tends to be better to use a classic cooking method such as pan-frying. One exception: Hard-boiled eggs are easier to make in the air fryer. Enter this herby egg sandwich.

ACTIVE TIME 15 minutes   TOTAL TIME 20 minutes   SERVES 4

Banana Bread Puddings

Bananas seem to go from just ripe to brown in seconds. Instead of throwing them away, mash the mottled bananas and transform them into this spoonable banana bread. Oat flour gives these breads a nuttier flavor and chewier texture (and more fiber!) than all-purpose would. To make your own, blend old-fashioned oats in a food processor until they become a fine flour, about 30 to 60 seconds.

ACTIVE TIME 20 minutes TOTAL TIME 50 minutes SERVES 4

1 tablespoon canola oil, plus more for brushing ramekins

4 large, very ripe bananas

2 large eggs, beaten

1 tablespoon pure maple syrup

1 teaspoon pure vanilla extract

3 tablespoons oat flour

¼ teaspoon kosher salt

½ teaspoon baking powder

⅓ cup plus 3 tablespoons large unsweetened coconut flakes, divided

½ cup whole pecans, plus 3 tablespoons, chopped

1. Lightly brush four 5- by 1-inch ramekins with oil.

2. In a large bowl, mash the bananas, then whisk in the eggs, maple syrup, vanilla and oil.

3. In a food processor, pulse together the oat flour, salt, baking powder, whole pecans and ⅓ cup coconut flakes until chopped (nuts and coconut should be in small pieces). Fold the flour mixture into the banana mixture.

4. Heat the air fryer to 335°F. Divide the batter among the prepared ramekins. Top each with the remaining 3 tablespoons coconut flakes and the chopped pecans.

5. Working in batches if needed, add the ramekins to the air-fryer basket and air-fry 6 minutes. Using tongs, rotate the ramekins, then air-fry until golden brown and cooked through, 7 to 8 minutes more. Let rest 3 minutes so the puddings will set before serving.

—

PER SERVING *About 390 calories, 24 g fat (6 g saturated fat), 7 g protein, 225 mg sodium, 42 g carbohydrates, 6 g fiber*

Spinach and Cheese Breakfast Pockets

While flaky apple hand pies are a fall favorite (see page 169), this savory twist can be enjoyed all year round and served for breakfast. Dedicate some time to meal prepping these pockets, and stash unbaked ones in the freezer. To enjoy later, fire up the air fryer to 350°F and air-fry until golden brown, 15 to 18 minutes.

ACTIVE TIME 20 minutes   TOTAL TIME 1 hour 20 minutes   SERVES 8

2   large eggs, divided

1   cup ricotta cheese

1   cup baby spinach, roughly chopped

1   cup fresh basil, chopped

¼   cup sun-dried tomatoes (about 9), finely chopped

¼   teaspoon red pepper flakes

    Kosher salt

2   refrigerated rolled pie crusts or 2 batches Best-Ever Pie Dough (see below)

    Oil, for brushing

    Sesame seeds, for topping

1. In a small bowl, whisk 1 egg with 1 tablespoon water; set aside.

2. In a medium bowl, combine the ricotta, spinach, basil, sun-dried tomatoes, red pepper flakes, remaining egg and ¼ teaspoon salt.

3. Unroll the pie crusts and cut each into 4 wedges. Divide the ricotta mixture among the wedges (about 3 tablespoons for each), placing the ricotta on one side, ½ inch from the edges. Fold the dough over the filling and press the edges with a fork to seal.

4. Heat the air fryer to 380°F. Brush the air-fryer basket with oil. Brush the tops of the dough with the egg mixture and sprinkle with sesame seeds. Working in batches, add 2 pieces at a time to the basket and air-fry until golden brown, 10 to 12 minutes.

—

PER SERVING *About 285 calories, 8 g fat (8 g saturated fat), 8 g protein, 370 mg sodium, 27 g carbohydrates, 1 g fiber*

Best-Ever Pie Dough

In a food processor, combine 1¼ cups **all-purpose flour**, 1½ teaspoons **sugar** and ½ teaspoon **kosher salt**. Add ½ cup (1 stick) **cold unsalted butter** (cut into small pieces and frozen 20 minutes); pulse until the mixture resembles coarse crumbs (slightly smaller than peas). Continue to pulse, adding 3 tablespoons **ice water**, until the dough is crumbly but holds together when squeezed. Pulse in more ice water, 1 teaspoon at a time, if necessary. Do not overmix. Transfer the dough onto a piece of plastic wrap and shape into a ½-inch-thick disk. Wrap tightly and refrigerate until firm, at least 1 hour or up to 2 days. Before using, roll dough into a 9-inch round.

Homemade Hash Browns

We tried a few different cooking methods but landed on this one: spreading shredded potatoes and onions out in the air-fryer basket to cook, then breaking them apart into smaller pieces right before serving. (P.S. Do not skip squeezing out the excess liquid — it is vital to ensure the potatoes brown up instead of steam and get soggy.)

ACTIVE TIME 10 minutes   TOTAL TIME 30 minutes   SERVES 4

3 tablespoons canola oil, plus more for brushing

Kosher salt and pepper

1 ¾ pounds large russet potatoes (2 to 3), peeled

1 small yellow onion

1 tablespoon all-purpose flour

Flaky sea salt, for sprinkling

1. In a large bowl, combine the oil, ¾ teaspoon salt and ½ teaspoon pepper. Using a grater or food processor fitted with a large grating hole, grate the potato and onion.

2. Heat the air fryer to 375°F. In two batches and using a lint-free kitchen towel, squeeze out the excess liquid from the potato mixture. Add to the bowl with the oil, sprinkle with the flour and toss to coat.

3. Liberally brush the air-fryer basket with oil, add the potatoes and use a spatula to spread them out to fill the basket. Air-fry until the potatoes begin to turn golden brown around the edges, 8 minutes.

4. Using a fork, fluff, quickly stir and expose the unbrowned pieces, leaving a slight border around the edge of the basket so the potatoes are not spread out too thin. Air-fry until the potatoes are deep golden brown and crisp on top and around the edges, 10 to 12 minutes more. Transfer to a platter in pieces and sprinkle with flaky salt.
—

PER SERVING *About 280 calories, 14 g fat (1 g saturated fat), 3 g protein, 370 mg sodium, 36 g carbohydrates, 3 g fiber*

air fryer advice

If you're using a toaster-oven-style basket that has many tiny holes or is made from stainless steel, place the potatoes on a quarter sheet pan brushed with oil in step 3.

TEST KITCHEN TIP
Adding the egg white helps the granola pieces clump together.

Sweet and Salty Granola Bark

Making granola from scratch allows you to customize your mix, which is essential for anyone with an allergy or dietary preference. Often, however, freshly baked granola is softer and chewier than what you'd get from the store. Not anymore: The high heat and intense air circulation help crisp up the crunchy clusters.

ACTIVE TIME 15 minutes   TOTAL TIME 45 minutes, plus cooling   SERVES 6

- 1 large egg white
- ½ cup pure maple syrup
- 1 teaspoon pure vanilla extract
- ¼ cup olive oil
- Kosher salt
- 1½ cups old-fashioned oats
- ½ cup roasted, salted almonds, coarsely chopped
- ¼ cup sunflower seeds
- ¼ cup all-purpose flour
- ¾ teaspoon ground cinnamon

1. In a small bowl, lightly beat the egg white with a fork; measure 1 tablespoon beaten egg white and set aside. Discard remaining egg white or save for another use.

2. Remove the insert from the bottom of the air-fryer basket. Cut a piece of parchment paper to line the insert.

3. In a small bowl, combine the maple syrup, vanilla, oil, ¼ teaspoon salt and reserved egg white. In a large bowl, combine the oats, almonds, sunflower seeds, flour and cinnamon. Add the maple syrup mixture to the dry ingredients and mix to combine.

4. Using the back of a spoon or wet hands, evenly press half of the mixture (1 ⅓ cups) onto the piece of parchment.

5. Heat the air fryer to 325°F. Carefully add the parchment-lined insert to the basket. Air-fry without disturbing until golden brown, 12 to 16 minutes.

6. Carefully transfer the granola bark to a wire rack and let cool at least 1 hour before breaking into chunks.

7. Repeat steps 4 through 6 with the remaining oat mixture. Store in an airtight container at room temperature for up to 1 week.

—

PER SERVING *About 335 calories, 22 g fat (2 g saturated fat), 7 g protein, 145 mg sodium, 30 g carbohydrates, 4 g fiber*

Tasty Toppers

Try one of these Test Kitchen combinations or get creative and mix and match as you please. All measurements apply to one slice of "toast."

COOL CUCUMBER
1 ½ tablespoons cottage cheese + mini cucumber slices + a drizzle of chili crisp

TRAIL MIX
1 tablespoon sunflower seed butter +
1 tablespoon granola

PARFAIT-STYLE
1 tablespoon Greek yogurt +
1 teaspoon jam +
1 teaspoon sliced almonds

Sweet Potato "Toasts"

Sweet Potato "Toasts"

Swap in slices of sweet potato for toasted bread and treat them as blank canvases for all your favorite toppings. Once air-fried — following our foolproof method — you should be able to eat them by hand.

ACTIVE TIME 5 minutes
TOTAL TIME 20 minutes
SERVES 4 or 5

1 large sweet potato (about 11 ounces), scrubbed and dried

Olive oil, for brushing

Kosher salt

1. Heat the air fryer to 390°F. Slice the ends off the sweet potato and cut lengthwise into ½-inch-thick slabs (about 5 slices). Brush both sides with oil and season with a pinch of salt.

2. Working in batches if needed, place the slices into the air-fryer basket and air-fry, flipping halfway through, until they are just tender but still hold their shape, 11 to 12 minutes. Top as desired.

—

PER SERVING (TOAST ONLY) *About 30 calories, 0 g fat (0 g saturated fat), 0 g protein, 20 mg sodium, 7 g carbohydrates, 1 g fiber*

Sriracha Bacon

Introduce a dash of hot sauce and a drizzle of something sweet and you take bacon to the next level. It is important to wait until the end of cooking to add any glazes to the air fryer in order to prevent your food from burning.

ACTIVE TIME 10 minutes
TOTAL TIME 40 minutes
SERVES 5

2 tablespoons pure maple syrup

2 tablespoons sriracha

10 slices thick-cut bacon

1. In a small bowl, whisk together the maple syrup and sriracha. Set aside.

2. Heat the air fryer to 325°F. Working in batches if needed, line the air-fryer basket with the bacon slices. Air-fry 10 minutes. Using tongs, flip the bacon and air-fry 8 minutes more.

3. Brush the maple-sriracha glaze onto the top of each slice of bacon and air-fry until golden and crispy, 1 minute more. Repeat as necessary with the remaining bacon and glaze.

—

PER SERVING *About 120 calories, 6.5 g fat (2 g saturated fat), 6 g protein, 495 mg sodium, 8 g carbohydrates, 0 g fiber*

chapter two

Apps and Snacks

The air fryer first caught everyone's eye when it turned out crispy, delicious versions of french fries and chicken wings sans the oil. Now we know it can do so much more! Think elegant stuffed mushrooms, cheesy game-day totchos and even deviled eggs.

RECIPES

Want a Buffalo sauce? Turn to page 43 for our variation, then toss with air-fried wings and cook until browned in spots.

Gochujang-Glazed Chicken Wings

Finger. Licking. Good. Once you've had air-fryer wings, we guarantee you'll never want them any other way. Follow our formula for chicken that is perfectly juicy on the inside and crispy on the outside — complete with an awesome sauce — that also works with your own signature seasonings.

ACTIVE TIME 10 minutes **TOTAL TIME** 50 minutes **SERVES** 4

2 pounds chicken wings, tips removed and wings split

Kosher salt

¼ cup gochujang

2 tablespoons mirin

1 tablespoon rice vinegar

1 tablespoon pure maple syrup

1 teaspoon toasted sesame oil

½ tablespoon grated peeled fresh ginger

½ clove garlic, grated

Sliced scallions and toasted sesame seeds, for topping

1. Pat the chicken wings dry and season with ⅛ teaspoon salt.

2. In a large bowl, combine the gochujang, mirin, vinegar, maple syrup, sesame oil, ginger and garlic.

3. Heat the air fryer to 400°F. Working in batches if needed, place the wings in the air-fryer basket and air-fry, turning with tongs halfway through cooking, until the skin is browned and the chicken is almost cooked through, 15 minutes. Transfer to a plate if working in batches.

4. Once all the wings have been air-fried, brush them with 3 tablespoons of the gochujang sauce and cook until browned in spots, 4 minutes more.

5. Transfer the wings to the bowl with the remaining sauce and toss to coat. Sprinkle with scallions and sesame seeds and serve immediately.

—

PER SERVING *About 355 calories, 20 g fat (5 g saturated fat), 26 g protein, 600 mg sodium, 17 g carbohydrates, 1 g fiber*

Smoky Chicken Wings

Before adding chicken to the air-fryer basket, toss with 1 tablespoon **smoked paprika**, 2 teaspoons **brown sugar**, ½ tablespoon **ancho chile powder**, ½ tablespoon **ground cumin**, ¼ teaspoon **coarsely cracked black pepper** and ¼ teaspoon **dry mustard**. Air-fry the chicken wings, turning with tongs halfway through cooking, until the skin is browned and the chicken is cooked through, 18 to 20 minutes. Serve immediately with ranch dressing for dipping.

TEST KITCHEN TIP
We opted for cream of coconut because it adds a much-needed sweetness to the dipping sauce; many brands of coconut cream are unsweetened.

Crispy Coconut Shrimp

A trio of panko, cornstarch and a quick blast in the air fryer delivers optimal and satisfying crispy breading. Extra-large shrimp can stand up to the longer cook time that the crunchy coating needs. If you're tempted to use less oil, don't try it. We experimented with decreasing the amount of oil but found the results lackluster.

ACTIVE TIME 20 minutes   **TOTAL TIME** 40 minutes   **SERVES** 4

FOR THE COCONUT-SCALLION DIPPING SAUCE

- ⅓ cup cream of coconut, warmed slightly if congealed
- 1 teaspoon lime zest plus 2 tablespoons fresh lime juice
- 1 teaspoon fish sauce
- 2 large scallions, finely chopped
- ¼ serrano chile, finely chopped

FOR THE SHRIMP

- ¾ cup panko
- 1 cup sweetened shredded coconut
- 3 tablespoons canola oil, plus more for brushing
- Kosher salt
- ⅓ cup cornstarch
- 1 teaspoon granulated garlic
- 1 large egg
- 1 pound extra-large tail-on peeled and deveined shrimp

1. Make the dipping sauce: In a small bowl, combine the cream of coconut, lime zest, lime juice, fish sauce, scallions and chopped serrano; set aside until ready to use. Keep any extra sauce in the fridge for up to 4 days.

2. Prepare the shrimp: In a shallow bowl, toss the panko, shredded coconut, oil and ½ teaspoon salt to combine, gently massaging the ingredients together. In a second shallow bowl, combine the cornstarch and granulated garlic. In a third shallow bowl, beat the egg with 1 tablespoon water. (Don't skip the water: It yields a fluffier egg and will incorporate air into your batter!)

3. Begin breading: Toss the shrimp in the cornstarch mixture and shake off any excess, then toss in the egg to fully coat. Working one at a time, remove the shrimp from the egg, letting the excess drip off, and coat in the coconut mixture, pressing gently to help the breading adhere; transfer to a plate and repeat with the remaining shrimp.

4. Heat the air fryer to 375°F. Brush the air-fryer basket with oil. Working in batches if needed, add the shrimp to the basket and air-fry 4 minutes. Using tongs, flip the shrimp and air-fry until golden brown, 4 minutes more. Serve the shrimp with the dipping sauce.

—

PER SERVING *About 465 calories, 21 g fat (8 g saturated fat), 27 g protein, 615 mg sodium, 43 g carbohydrates, 3 g fiber*

TEST KITCHEN TIP
The biggest challenge is the batter, which can drip off and burn at the bottom of your appliance. Thanks to a tempura-inspired technique, ours is light and airy.

Buffalo Cauliflower Bites

These are an ideal vegetarian variation on chicken wings for game day.
Simply toss these bites with Buffalo sauce, serve with a cool dipping sauce
and try not to eat them all before halftime.

ACTIVE TIME 20 minutes   **TOTAL TIME** 45 minutes   **SERVES** 4

FOR THE DIPPING SAUCE

- ¾ cup sour cream
- 2 teaspoons fresh lemon juice
- Kosher salt and pepper
- ½ teaspoon buffalo wing sauce (we used Frank's RedHot)
- 1 large scallion, finely chopped
- 1½ ounces blue cheese, crumbled (about ⅓ cup)

FOR THE BUFFALO SAUCE

- ⅓ cup buffalo wing sauce (we used Frank's RedHot)
- 1 tablespoon canola oil
- ½ teaspoon honey

FOR THE CAULIFLOWER

- ½ cup rice flour
- ¼ cup cornstarch
- ¼ teaspoon baking powder
- ¼ teaspoon kosher salt
- ½ cup plus 2 tablespoons cold seltzer
- 1 2-pound head cauliflower, trimmed and cut into 1½-inch florets
- Canola oil, for brushing
- Celery sticks, for serving

1. Make the dipping sauce: In a medium bowl, combine all the ingredients; refrigerate until ready to use.

2. Make the Buffalo sauce: In a large bowl, whisk together all the ingredients; set aside.

3. Prepare the cauliflower: Heat the air fryer to 400°F. In a large bowl, whisk together the rice flour, cornstarch, baking powder and salt. Whisk in the seltzer. Add the cauliflower and toss to coat.

4. Brush the air-fryer basket with oil. Working in batches if needed, add the cauliflower to the basket in a single layer. Air-fry, shaking the basket after 10 minutes and continuing to cook until crispy, 15 minutes total. Transfer to a plate. If working in batches, when the second batch is done, leave in the basket and top with the first batch of cauliflower; air-fry 2 minutes to reheat.

5. Transfer the cauliflower to the bowl of Buffalo sauce and toss to coat. Serve immediately with the dipping sauce and celery.

—

PER SERVING *About 285 calories, 16 g fat (6 g saturated fat), 6 g protein, 1,075 mg sodium, 31 g carbohydrates, 3 g fiber*

TEST KITCHEN TIP
For the most satisfying crunch, do not overcrowd your air fryer basket. Take the time to work in batches. (Trust us, the extra time is worth it!)

Spiced Snack Mix

Whenever you're expecting company, make a batch of this party mix.
Your whole house will smell amazing — buttery, cheesy and oh so savory.
(P.S. Who knew cheese crackers taste so much better air-fried?!)

ACTIVE TIME 5 minutes   **TOTAL TIME** 25 minutes   **SERVES** 8

3 ½ cups mini pretzels

2 cups toasted corn squares cereal (we used Corn Chex)

2 cups cheese crackers

6 tablespoons unsalted butter, melted

3 tablespoons pure maple syrup

¼ cup sunflower seeds

2 tablespoons white sesame seeds

1 tablespoon black sesame seeds

1 tablespoon dried minced onion

1 teaspoon caraway seeds

1 teaspoon dried parsley

½ teaspoon cracked black pepper

1. Heat the air fryer to 300°F. In a large bowl, toss the pretzels, cereal and crackers with the melted butter and maple syrup to coat. Toss with the sunflower seeds, sesame seeds, onion, caraway seeds, parsley and pepper.

2. Working in batches if needed, arrange the snack mix in an even layer in the air-fryer basket and air-fry, shaking the basket halfway through, until lightly toasted in spots, about 10 minutes. Let cool, then serve or store in an airtight container for up to 1 week.

—

PER SERVING (1 CUP) *About 270 calories, 15 g fat (6 g saturated fat), 5 g protein, 245 mg sodium, 31 g carbohydrates, 2 g fiber*

Mozzarella Sticks

We cracked the code on how to get pretty close to achieving authentic deep-fried texture without a ton of added oil or a complete mess. Toasting the panko in the air fryer first, double-breading the cheese sticks and popping them into the freezer to help everything firm up did the trick.

ACTIVE TIME 20 minutes **TOTAL TIME** 30 minutes, plus chilling **SERVES** 6

1 ½ cups panko

2 tablespoons olive oil, plus more for brushing

6 mozzarella string cheese sticks

¼ cup all-purpose flour

2 large eggs

Kosher salt

1 teaspoon garlic powder

½ teaspoon red pepper flakes

½ teaspoon dried oregano

Warmed marinara sauce, for serving

1. Heat the air fryer to 370°F. In a medium shallow bowl, combine the panko and oil. Transfer the crumb mixture to a piece of aluminum foil, slightly fold up the sides to create a shallow "boat" and place in the air-fryer basket. Air-fry, stirring halfway through, until the crumbs are evenly golden brown, 4 to 6 minutes. Let cool slightly.

2. Meanwhile, line a small tray or baking sheet with parchment paper. Halve the cheese sticks crosswise. Place the flour in a small, shallow bowl. In a second shallow bowl, beat the eggs with a pinch of salt to combine.

3. Transfer the cooled panko to a food processor, adding the garlic powder, ¾ teaspoon salt, red pepper flakes and oregano. Pulse until finely ground; transfer to a shallow bowl.

4. Begin breading: Working with a few cheese sticks at a time, lightly coat in the flour, then in the egg mixture (letting any excess drip off), and then roll in the panko mixture to evenly coat. Place on the prepared tray. Coat the cheese sticks in the egg mixture a second time, followed by another coating in the panko. Freeze for at least 1 hour or up to 4 hours.

5. During the last few minutes of chilling, heat the air fryer to 390°F. Lightly brush the mozzarella sticks with oil, then brush the basket with oil. Working in batches if needed, arrange the mozzarella sticks in a single layer in the basket, spacing them apart so they don't touch. Air-fry until golden brown and crisp, 5 to 6 minutes. Serve with marinara sauce.

—

PER SERVING *About 220 calories, 9 g fat (3 g saturated fat), 13 g protein, 525 mg sodium, 21 g carbohydrates, 1 g fiber*

TEST KITCHEN TIP
Vary the fillings, subbing in shredded pork or ground beef, or switch up the toppings with guac or pickled veggies.

Chicken Taquitos

These rolled tacos feature a creamy, cheesy enchilada-style chicken filling that becomes melty and downright delicious. Assembled corn tortillas crisp up in an air fryer faster than in the oven.

ACTIVE TIME 10 minutes   **TOTAL TIME** 25 minutes   **SERVES** 4 to 6

4   ounces cream cheese, at room temperature

⅓   cup red enchilada sauce

¼   cup sour cream

  Kosher salt and pepper

3   cups finely shredded white-meat rotisserie chicken

6   ounces Colby Jack cheese, coarsely grated

½   cup fresh cilantro, chopped, plus more for topping

12   small corn tortillas

  Olive oil, for brushing

  Pico de gallo, sour cream and crumbled cotija cheese, for topping

1. Heat the air fryer to 400°F.

2. In a large bowl, combine the cream cheese, enchilada sauce, sour cream and ½ teaspoon each salt and pepper. Fold in the chicken, Colby Jack and cilantro.

3. In batches, place the tortillas on a microwave-safe plate and cover with a damp paper towel. Microwave until warm and pliable, 30 to 60 seconds.

4. Brush the air-fryer basket with oil. Divide the chicken mixture among the warmed tortillas (scant ¼ cup each), roll up tightly, and place in the basket, seam sides down. Brush the tortillas with oil and air-fry until golden brown and crisp, 8 to 10 minutes.

5. Transfer the taquitos to a platter and top with pico de gallo, sour cream, cotija and more cilantro.

—

PER SERVING *About 405 calories, 21.5 g fat (11.5 g saturated fat), 29 g protein, 705 mg sodium, 21 g carbohydrates, 3 g fiber*

TEST KITCHEN TIP
Take one extra step for a pretty presentation: Transfer the yolk mixture to a resealable plastic bag, snip a corner and pipe the filling into the egg whites.

Deviled Eggs

Once we realized that the air fryer is an easy way to prep a batch of hard-boiled eggs (see the Green Goddess Sandwiches on page 25), we knew we had to try our favorite snack. It's essentially a three-step crowd-pleasing app ready to go. Begin with the basics, mixing yolks with mayonnaise, lemon juice, Dijon (to add creaminess) and hot sauce (for a hint of heat and acidity). Then decide on your toppings — crumbled bacon, fresh herbs, crushed potato chips, you name it.

ACTIVE TIME 15 minutes   **TOTAL TIME** 30 minutes   **SERVES** 6

6   **large eggs**

    Ice water, for cooling

2   **tablespoons mayonnaise**

1   **teaspoon fresh lemon juice**

1   **teaspoon Dijon mustard**

½   **teaspoon hot sauce**

    Kosher salt and pepper

    Crumbled bacon, sliced scallions and chopped fresh chives, parsley and dill, for topping

1. Heat the air fryer to 275°F. Place the eggs in the air-fryer basket and air-fry 15 minutes. Immediately transfer the eggs to a bowl of ice water to cool for a few minutes, then peel and halve lengthwise.

2. Transfer the egg yolks to a small bowl and mash with the mayonnaise, lemon juice, mustard, hot sauce and ⅛ teaspoon each salt and pepper. Spoon into the egg whites and sprinkle with toppings as desired.

—

PER SERVING *About 110 calories, 8.5 g fat (2 g saturated fat), 6 g protein, 160 mg sodium, 1 g carbohydrates, 0 g fiber*

Crispy Ranch Pickle Chips

A perennial state fair favorite, deep-fried pickles are a crispy, puckery, straight-up-fun snack. This lighter variation is served with a Greek yogurt dip in lieu of sour cream. Incorporating ranch seasoning into the breading situation intensifies the flavor.

ACTIVE TIME 20 minutes   **TOTAL TIME** 50 minutes   **SERVES** 6

1 1-ounce packet ranch seasoning (about 4 tablespoons), divided

2 large eggs

⅓ cup all-purpose flour

1 cup panko

6 dill pickles (about 12 ounces), sliced ¼ inch thick

Oil, for brushing

½ cup whole milk Greek yogurt

1 tablespoon fresh flat-leaf parsley, chopped

1. Place 2 teaspoons of the ranch seasoning in a small bowl and set aside. Line a baking sheet with parchment paper.

2. Beat the eggs in a shallow bowl and place the flour in a separate bowl. In a third bowl, combine the panko and remaining ranch seasoning (about 3 tablespoons plus 1 teaspoon).

3. Heat the air fryer to 390°F. Pat the pickle slices dry and lightly coat in the flour, then in the eggs (letting any excess drip off), and finally in the panko mixture, pressing gently to help adhere. Transfer to the prepared baking sheet.

4. Lightly brush the air-fryer basket with oil. Working in batches if needed, arrange the pickles in a single layer and air-fry until golden brown and crisp, 10 to 12 minutes.

5. In the small bowl with the reserved ranch seasoning, whisk in the yogurt and parsley to combine. Serve the dipping sauce with the pickles.

—

PER SERVING *About 150 calories, 4 g fat (1 g saturated fat), 7 g protein, 865 mg sodium, 20 g carbohydrates, 1 g fiber*

Jalapeño Poppers

Now you can easily make this bar-menu staple at home. Once you stuff the chiles, chill them in the fridge for a few minutes. This helps to prevent the scallion-cheese mixture from oozing out in the air fryer. (Trust us, that's not a mess you want to clean up!)

ACTIVE TIME 10 minutes **TOTAL TIME** 20 minutes **SERVES** 4 to 6

4 ounces cream cheese, at room temperature

2 ounces extra-sharp Cheddar cheese, coarsely grated

1 scallion, finely chopped

Dash of hot sauce

6 medium to large jalapeños

Oil, for brushing

1. In a medium bowl, combine the cream cheese, Cheddar, scallion and hot sauce until smooth. Transfer to a resealable plastic bag. Halve the jalapeños lengthwise and scrape out the seeds with a small spoon.

2. Heat the air fryer to 375°F. Snip off one corner of the bag and pipe the cheese mixture into the jalapeño halves. Lightly brush the air-fryer basket with oil and arrange the poppers in a single layer. Working in batches if needed, air-fry until the tops are browned, 6 to 7 minutes. (Make sure to brush the basket with oil between batches.)

—

PER SERVING *About 135 calories, 12 g fat (7 g saturated fat), 4 g protein, 145 mg sodium, 3 g carbohydrates, 1 g fiber*

TEST KITCHEN TIP
Keep a close eye on these nests — they cook so quickly! Break one open after your first batch is done. If it's dry, shorten the air-frying time for your next batch by 30 seconds or so.

Kale and White Cheddar Nests

Introducing our favorite way to get our greens in. Made with a mix of all-purpose and almond flours, this light and delicate appetizer browns up beautifully in the air fryer. Take extra care while flipping, so you don't lose any bits of kale or Cheddar in the grooves of the grate.

ACTIVE TIME 25 minutes   **TOTAL TIME** 40 minutes   **SERVES** 24

8	ounces Tuscan kale (about ½ bunch), stemmed and leaves halved lengthwise, then thinly sliced crosswise
1	tablespoon olive oil
	Kosher salt and pepper
2	large eggs
1	scallion, finely chopped
2	cloves garlic, grated
½	cup almond flour
½	teaspoon baking powder
1½	tablespoons all-purpose flour
4	ounces extra-sharp white Cheddar cheese, grated

1. Cut a piece of parchment paper large enough to fit into the air-fryer basket (leaving enough room around the edges to allow for air circulation); set aside. Heat the air fryer to 400°F. In a large bowl, rub the kale with the oil and ½ teaspoon salt. Add to the basket and air-fry until wilted, 1 minute; transfer back to the large bowl and let cool.

2. In a medium bowl, whisk together the eggs, scallion and garlic. In a small bowl, whisk the almond flour, baking powder and all-purpose flour to combine. Fold the egg mixture, flour mixture and cheese into the kale.

3. Line the basket with the prepared piece of parchment and drop in tablespoonfuls of the kale mixture, spacing them 1 inch apart. Working in batches if needed, air-fry until the nests start to turn golden brown, about 4 minutes. Using a small offset spatula or fork, carefully flip the nests and air-fry 1 minute more. Serve immediately.

—

PER SERVING (4 NESTS) *About 195 calories, 14 g fat (6 g saturated fat), 8 g protein, 375 mg sodium, 8 g carbohydrates, 4 g fiber*

Totchos

If you haven't attempted to air-fry frozen foods (read: fries, nuggets or onion rings), now is the time. No, really, put this cookbook down, head to the nearest grocery store's freezer section and add everything to your cart. Just kidding. But we're serious about these fully loaded tots. Upgrade store-bought spuds with dried spices and a generous sprinkling of cheese.

ACTIVE TIME 15 minutes **TOTAL TIME** 35 minutes **SERVES** 8

2	pounds frozen potato tots
1	teaspoon chili powder
½	teaspoon ground cumin
½	teaspoon ground coriander
⅛	teaspoon cayenne
1½	cups finely grated extra-sharp Cheddar cheese
	Avocado Dip (see below)

1. Heat the air fryer to 400°F. In a large bowl, toss the tots with the chili powder, cumin, coriander and cayenne.

2. Working in batches if needed, arrange the tots in a single layer in the air-fryer basket and air-fry 20 minutes.

3. Transfer half of the tots to a small platter and sprinkle with half of the Cheddar. Top with the remaining tots and cheese, then cover with aluminum foil for about 30 seconds to melt the cheese. Serve immediately with Avocado Dip.

—

PER SERVING *About 270 calories, 15 g fat (4 g saturated fat), 6 g protein, 665 mg sodium, 27 g carbohydrates, 3 g fiber*

Avocado Dip

Heat the air fryer to 400°F. In the air-fryer basket, toss together 2 small **poblano peppers**, 2 cloves **garlic** (not peeled), 1 small **jalapeño**, ½ medium **onion** (halved) and 1 tablespoon **olive oil**. Air-fry, turning the peppers once halfway through, until the vegetables are deeply charred, 6 to 8 minutes. Let cool, then use a paper towel to remove any skins and seeds. Transfer the vegetables to a blender along with 2 ripe **avocados**, 1 bunch fresh **cilantro**, ¼ cup fresh **lime juice**, ¼ cup **water** and ½ teaspoon **kosher salt** and puree until smooth, adding an additional 1 tablespoon water if needed.

TEST KITCHEN TIP
We love to sprinkle these on top of salads and soups too! Air-fry chickpeas for 10 minutes once completely cool to crisp them up again.

Parmesan Chickpeas

Transform a can of chickpeas into a crunchy protein-packed snack. Take the time to dry the chickpeas (and discard any loose skins) before adding them to the air fryer. You will definitely notice the difference! We tossed the beans with some cheese and lemon zest, but you can also enjoy them with just a hint of salt and pepper.

ACTIVE TIME 10 minutes **TOTAL TIME** 25 minutes **SERVES** 8

2   **15-ounce cans chickpeas, drained and rinsed**

2   **tablespoons olive oil**

  Kosher salt and pepper

¼   **cup grated Parmesan cheese**

1   **lemon**

1. Heat the air fryer to 400°F. Transfer the chickpeas to a kitchen towel and pat dry, discarding any loose skins. Transfer the chickpeas to a large bowl, drizzle with the oil and season with ¼ teaspoon each salt and pepper.

2. Add the chickpeas to the air-fryer basket and air-fry, without disturbing, 14 minutes. Shake the basket, sprinkle the chickpeas with the cheese and shake again. Air-fry until crisp, 2 minutes more.

3. Grate the zest of the lemon on top, shake to toss, then transfer the chickpeas to a serving bowl. They will continue to crisp as they cool; wait at least 10 minutes before eating them.

—

PER SERVING (¼ CUP) *About 130 calories, 6 g fat (1 g saturated fat), 5 g protein, 245 mg sodium, 16 g carbohydrates, 4 g fiber*

Sourdough- and Gruyère-Stuffed Mushrooms

This elegant appetizer really puts your air fryer to work. First, it's toasting slices of sourdough, so you can use homemade breadcrumbs. Then, it's cooking the mushroom stems while the caps marinate. Finally, it turns all these individual components into one tasty starter — complete with melty cheese, freshly toasted breadcrumbs and a hint of fresh herbs. It's a little fussy but worth the effort.

ACTIVE TIME 20 minutes   **TOTAL TIME** 45 minutes   **SERVES** 4

20 cremini mushrooms,
    1 3/4- to 2-inch diameter
    (about 12 ounces total)

 2 tablespoons plus
    2 teaspoons olive oil,
    divided

 2 cloves garlic, finely grated,
    divided

 1 teaspoon fresh thyme

    Kosher salt and pepper

 1 slice sourdough bread
    (2 ounces), cut into
    1 1/2-inch strips

 3 tablespoons sour cream

 3 scallions, dark green
    parts only, finely chopped
    (about 1/4 cup)

 4 ounces Gruyère cheese,
    coarsely grated (about
    1 1/4 cups)

 3 tablespoons fresh flat-leaf
    parsley, chopped

1. Remove the stems from the mushrooms and reserve. In a large bowl, mix 2 tablespoons of the oil with half of the garlic, the thyme and 1/4 teaspoon salt. Add the mushroom caps, toss to coat and set aside to marinate.

2. Heat the air fryer to 330°F. Brush both sides of the bread strips with 1 teaspoon of the oil and air-fry, flipping halfway through, until golden brown and crisp, 7 to 8 minutes. Let cool.

3. Heat the air fryer to 345°F. Trim and discard the tough ends from the reserved mushroom stems. Toss the stems with the remaining 1 teaspoon oil and a pinch of salt. Air-fry until tender, 6 minutes. Transfer to a cutting board and finely chop. Crush the cooled toasted bread into coarse crumbs.

4. In a medium bowl, combine the sour cream, scallion greens, mushroom stems, remaining garlic, 1/4 teaspoon salt and 1/8 teaspoon pepper. Fold in the breadcrumbs, then the cheese and parsley.

5. Heat the air fryer to 350°F. Stuff the mushroom caps with the filling mixture, packing it firmly inside each cap. Working in batches if needed, add the mushroom caps to the air-fryer basket and air-fry until the mushrooms are tender and the stuffing is golden brown and bubbly, 8 to 10 minutes. Let cool slightly before serving.

—

PER SERVING (5 MUSHROOMS) *About 275 calories, 20 g fat (7.5 g saturated fat), 12 g protein, 565 mg sodium, 12 g carbohydrates, 1 g fiber*

Shortcut Scallion Pancakes

Traditional recipes for this takeout favorite usually require kneading plus at least 30 to 45 minutes of resting time. We save time by making the most of store-bought dumpling wrappers. Sprinkle with sliced scallions, stack them and roll into thin savory pancakes.

ACTIVE TIME 30 minutes **TOTAL TIME** 45 minutes **SERVES** 4

¼ cup low-sodium soy sauce

2 tablespoons rice vinegar

2 teaspoons sambal oelek

1 teaspoon sugar

1 2-inch piece fresh ginger, peeled and cut into matchsticks

1 14-ounce package round white dumpling wrappers

¼ cup toasted sesame oil

Canola oil, for brushing

8 scallions, chopped (about 1 ½ cups), plus more for topping

1. In a small bowl, whisk together the soy sauce, rice vinegar, sambal oelek and sugar; stir in the ginger and set aside.

2. Place 1 dumpling wrapper on a cutting board. Brush the top with some of the sesame oil and scatter 2 teaspoons scallions on top. Top with a second dumpling wrapper, pressing your fingertips firmly straight down into the wrapper a few times to dimple and adhere to the previous layer. Repeat with the remaining wrappers, sesame oil and scallions to make a total of 8 stacks of 6 wrappers each.

3. Heat the air fryer to 400°F. Brush both sides of the stacks liberally with canola oil. Place 4 stacks in the air-fryer basket, spacing them so they don't touch. Air-fry 3 ½ minutes. Using tongs, flip and air-fry until golden brown and crispy, 3 to 4 minutes more. Repeat with the remaining stacks.

4. Sprinkle the pancakes with more scallions and serve with the ginger-chile sauce for dipping.

—

PER SERVING (2 PANCAKES) *About 215 calories, 7.5 g fat (1 g saturated fat), 6 g protein, 640 mg sodium, 30 g carbohydrates, 1 g fiber*

TEST KITCHEN TIP

Shape the potato mixture into a triangle in the center of the dough, then stretch the top portion of dough before folding over and pinching the edges.

Potato Samosas

Between its savory spiced potato filling and its perfectly flaky, crisp crust, there is so much to love about this popular South Asian pastry. We hacked the air fryer so you can melt butter and sauté the filling without worrying about things falling through the cracks (literally). Just remove the air-fryer insert in a basket-style air fryer or use a mini sheet pan in your toaster-oven-style air fryer.

ACTIVE TIME 1 hour 10 minutes **TOTAL TIME** 1 hour 20 minutes **SERVES** 16

2 tablespoons unsalted butter

1 pound large Yukon gold potatoes, peeled and cut into 1-inch cubes

1 small yellow onion, finely chopped

Kosher salt

½ teaspoon brown mustard seeds

1½ teaspoons cumin seeds

¾ teaspoon garam masala

½ teaspoon ground turmeric

1½ teaspoons finely grated peeled fresh ginger

½ teaspoon fresh lemon juice

½ small serrano chile, finely chopped

2 tablespoons fresh cilantro, chopped

2 refrigerated rolled pie crusts or 2 batches Best-Ever Pie Dough (page 29)

1 large egg, beaten

Canola oil, for brushing

Store-bought chutney, for serving

1. Remove the insert from the air-fryer basket. Heat the air fryer to 400°F.

2. Add the butter to the air-fryer basket and swirl to melt; add the potatoes, onion and 1 teaspoon salt and toss. Air-fry until the edges of the potatoes begin to turn golden brown, 5 minutes. Add the mustard seeds, cumin seeds, garam masala, turmeric and ½ cup water. Air-fry, shaking or stirring every 4 minutes and adding an additional tablespoon of water at a time if the mixture dries out, until the potatoes are tender, 12 to 16 minutes total.

3. Transfer the potato mixture to a large bowl and mash well. Stir in the ginger, lemon juice, serrano and cilantro. Set aside to cool.

4. Unroll one of the pie crusts and cut out 16 3-inch squares, rerolling scraps as necessary. Working with 8 squares at a time, brush the edges with the beaten egg and top each with about 1 tablespoon of the potato mixture. Fold in half to make a triangle, pinching the edges together with your fingers, then seal the edges with a fork.

5. Replace the air-fryer insert in the basket and heat the air fryer to 370°F. Brush the tops of the assembled samosas with the beaten egg. Brush the basket with oil, add the samosas and air-fry until golden brown, 8 to 10 minutes. Using tongs, flip the samosas, then air-fry until the bottoms are lightly golden brown, 2 minutes more. Repeat steps 4 and 5 with the remaining pie crust, beaten egg and filling.

—

PER SERVING (1 SAMOSA) *About 145 calories, 8 g fat (3.5 g saturated fat), 2 g protein, 260 mg sodium, 17 g carbohydrates, 0.5 g fiber*

chapter three

Mains

Conquer your weeknight dinnertime game plan and use your air fryer to get a meal on the table stat! Prepare perfectly cooked steaks or crispy chicken cutlets while whipping up sides separately, and you'll speed up your cook time so you can dig in and enjoy sooner.

RECIPES

Tandoori-Style Chicken

Traditionally, this Indian dish is cooked in a cylindrical clay oven called a tandoor. As a result, the chicken is juicy and tender with a crisp, golden-brown exterior and a deliciously smoky taste. Our version uses a spiced marinade and an air fryer to achieve a similar texture and flavor. To deepen that flavor, marinate the bone-in chicken pieces for closer to four hours.

ACTIVE TIME 15 minutes   TOTAL TIME 35 minutes, plus marinating   SERVES 4

½ cup plain yogurt

1 tablespoon fresh lemon juice, plus lemon wedges for serving

1 tablespoon paprika

½ tablespoon grated peeled fresh ginger

2 cloves garlic, grated

1 teaspoon garam masala

½ teaspoon ground turmeric

½ teaspoon ground coriander

¼ teaspoon cayenne

4 small chicken legs, each split into 2 parts

1 tablespoon olive oil, plus more for brushing

Kosher salt and pepper

2 small red onions, cut into ½-inch-thick wedges

Fresh cilantro, for topping

1. In a medium bowl, whisk together the yogurt, lemon juice, paprika, ginger, garlic, garam masala, turmeric, coriander and cayenne. Add the chicken, turn to coat and let sit at least 20 minutes or up to 4 hours.

2. Heat the air fryer to 400°F. Brush the air-fryer basket with oil. Remove the chicken from the marinade, season with ½ teaspoon salt and arrange, skin side up, in the basket. Air-fry 12 minutes.

3. Toss the onions with 1 tablespoon oil and ¼ teaspoon each salt and pepper and scatter around the chicken pieces. Air-fry until the chicken is cooked through (165°F) and the onions are golden brown and tender, 8 to 12 minutes more.

4. Transfer the chicken and onions to a platter along with the lemon wedges and sprinkle with cilantro.

—

PER SERVING *About 440 calories, 23.5 g fat (6 g saturated fat), 48 g protein, 565 mg sodium, 7 g carbohydrates, 2 g fiber*

love your leftovers

Shred any extra chicken and transfer to an airtight container — along with any additional onions — to keep in the fridge. Reheat and serve on top of warmed naan with labneh or Greek yogurt.

Chicken Schnitzel

Schnitzel refers to any kind of meat that has been pounded thin, coated with breadcrumbs and pan-fried. This recipe uses boneless, skinless chicken breasts and an air fryer in lieu of a skillet. The quality of the finished dish hasn't been sacrificed — juicy on the inside with a shatteringly crisp exterior — but you're using a lot less oil. Serve it with salad for an extra-pretty presentation.

ACTIVE TIME 35 minutes   TOTAL TIME 35 minutes   SERVES 4

- **4 5-ounce boneless, skinless chicken breasts**
- **1 tablespoon fresh lemon juice, plus lemon wedges for serving**
- **Kosher salt and pepper**
- **1 large egg plus 1 large egg white**
- **¼ cup all-purpose flour**
- **1 cup panko**
- **Olive oil, for brushing**
- **Tomato-Arugula Salad (see below), for serving**

1. Wrap a meat mallet or heavy can in plastic wrap. Pound the chicken breasts in a sliding motion, from the centers outward, until ¼ inch thick. Rub with the lemon juice, then season with ½ teaspoon each salt and pepper.

2. Beat the egg and egg white in a shallow bowl. Place the flour and panko in two separate shallow bowls. Working one at a time, coat the cutlets first in the flour, then in the egg, then in the panko, pressing gently to help the panko adhere.

3. Heat the air fryer to 400°F. Brush the air-fryer basket with oil, then brush each chicken breast with ½ tablespoon oil. Working in batches if needed, place in the basket, spacing them apart so they don't touch. Air-fry 9 minutes. Using tongs, flip the chicken and air-fry until golden brown, fully cooked through (165°F) and crispy, 3 minutes more. Serve with lemon wedges and Tomato-Arugula Salad.

—

PER SERVING *About 510 calories, 31 g fat (10 g saturated fat), 36 g protein, 170 mg sodium, 22 g carbohydrates, 1 g fiber*

Tomato-Arugula Salad

In a medium bowl, whisk together 2 tablespoons **olive oil**, 1 tablespoon **red wine vinegar** and ½ teaspoon each **kosher salt** and **pepper**. Stir in 1 small **shallot** (thinly sliced). Add 1 pint **grape or cherry tomatoes** (halved) and toss to combine; fold in 2 cups **baby arugula** and ¼ cup small **basil leaves**. Spoon the salad over the schnitzel.

TEST KITCHEN TIP
Before dredging the cutlets, toss them in a splash of lemon juice, which helps to tenderize the meat.

Chicken Parm

Take this Italian American favorite from good to amazing. For a beautifully crunchy coating that has larger extra-crispy bits, add oil and just the right amount of cheese to your panko breading. Then let the air fryer work its magic! P.S. A side of garlic bread (page 113) is a must.

ACTIVE TIME 20 minutes   TOTAL TIME 1 hour   SERVES 4

½ cup all-purpose flour

2 large eggs

1 teaspoon granulated garlic

Kosher salt and pepper

2 cups panko

⅓ cup plus 2 tablespoons grated Parmesan cheese, divided

3 tablespoons olive oil, plus more for brushing

2 8-ounce boneless, skinless chicken breasts, trimmed and split into cutlets

2 tablespoons fresh lemon juice

1 cup marinara sauce

¼ cup fresh basil, roughly chopped

6 ounces mozzarella cheese (do not use fresh), coarsely grated

Chopped fresh basil, for topping

1. Place the flour in a shallow bowl. In a second shallow bowl, beat together the eggs, garlic, 2 tablespoons water and ¾ teaspoon salt. In a third shallow bowl, combine the panko with ⅓ cup Parmesan and toss with the oil.

2. Pound each chicken cutlet to an even thickness. In a large bowl, toss with the lemon juice to coat. Dip each cutlet in the flour, then in the egg mixture (letting the excess drip off), then in the panko mixture, patting to adhere. Transfer to a parchment-lined plate.

3. Heat the air fryer to 360°F. Brush the air-fryer basket liberally with oil and add 2 cutlets. Air-fry until beginning to turn golden brown, 6 minutes. Using tongs, flip and air-fry until golden brown and cooked through (165°F), 7 to 9 minutes more. Transfer to a new plate. Repeat with the remaining cutlets.

4. Return 2 cooked cutlets to the basket and spoon 4 tablespoons marinara on top of each. Sprinkle each with 1 tablespoon basil, then with mozzarella and Parmesan. Heat the air fryer to 400°F. Air-fry until the cheese is bubbling and beginning to brown, 2 to 3 minutes. Repeat with the remaining cutlets, marinara, basil, mozzarella and Parmesan. Sprinkle with parsley.

—

PER SERVING *About 690 calories, 32 g fat (11 g saturated fat), 45 g protein, 1,240 mg sodium, 52 g carbohydrates, 3 g fiber*

Roasted Kale and Mushrooms

page 117

Mustard- and Spice-Rubbed Pork Tenderloin

Try tender, juicy, perfectly cooked pork tenderloin coated with a simple blend of spices or instead try a medley of herbs for fresh, bright flavor. Both options transform a budget-friendly cut of meat into a wow-worthy meal.

ACTIVE TIME 15 minutes   TOTAL TIME 35 minutes   SERVES 4

1 ½ teaspoons sweet paprika

1 teaspoon smoked paprika

1 teaspoon ground coriander

½ teaspoon ground cardamom

Kosher salt and pepper

1 tablespoon Dijon mustard

1 1 ¼-pound pork tenderloin, cut in half crosswise

1 tablespoon olive oil

1. In a small bowl, combine the sweet and smoked paprikas, coriander, cardamom, ¾ teaspoon salt and ½ teaspoon pepper. Brush the mustard evenly over the pork, then sprinkle with the spice mixture, pressing to adhere.

2. Heat the air fryer to 400°F. Add the pork tenderloin to the air-fryer basket and air-fry the pork tenderloin until fully cooked (145°F), 15 to 18 minutes. Transfer to a cutting board and let rest at least 10 minutes before slicing.

—

PER SERVING *About 200 calories, 8 g fat (1 g saturated fat), 29 g protein, 510 mg sodium, 2 g carbohydrates, 1 g fiber*

Lemony Garlic and Herb Pork Tenderloin

In a small bowl, combine ¼ cup finely chopped fresh **mixed herbs** (parsley, mint, chives, rosemary and thyme), 1 clove **garlic** (finely grated), 1 teaspoon **lemon zest**, ¼ teaspoon **red pepper flakes** and ¼ cup **olive oil**. Heat the air fryer to 400°F. Add the pork tenderloin to the air-fryer basket and air-fry 7 minutes. Brush the pork with the herb-oil mixture, then air-fry until fully cooked (145°F), 8 to 11 minutes more. Transfer to a cutting board and let rest at least 10 minutes before slicing.

Garlicky Honey Butter Pork Chops

Pork chops are generally a lean cut of meat that can easily overcook or dry out. Here, it's best to opt for thick, bone-in chops; the bone helps slow down how fast the meat cooks, giving you more time to achieve a picture-perfect "sear" in the air fryer.

ACTIVE TIME 5 minutes   TOTAL TIME 25 minutes   SERVES 4

2 tablespoons butter, melted

2 teaspoons honey

2 cloves garlic, smashed

1 teaspoon thyme leaves, plus 4 sprigs

4 1½-inch pork rib chops (about 2 pounds total)

   Kosher salt and pepper

1. In a small bowl, combine the butter, honey, garlic and thyme leaves. Season the pork chops with ½ teaspoon each salt and pepper.

2. Heat the air fryer to 400°F. Working in batches if needed, add the pork chops to the air-fryer basket and air-fry 5 minutes. Brush the honey butter all over the pork chops, add the thyme sprigs and air-fry until the chops are just cooked through (145°F), 10 minutes more. Transfer to a cutting board and let rest at least 5 minutes before serving.

—

PER SERVING *About 415 calories, 28 g fat (11 g saturated fat), 36 g protein, 380 mg sodium, 4 g carbohydrates, 0 g fiber*

make it a meal

Serve pork with a quick side salad: In a large bowl, whisk together 2 tablespoons **lemon juice**, 2 tablespoons **olive oil**, 2 teaspoons **Dijon mustard**, ½ teaspoon **kosher salt** and ¼ teaspoon **pepper**. Add 2 stalks **celery** (thinly sliced), 1 **Bartlett pear** (cored and thinly sliced), 1 bulb **fennel** (cored and thinly sliced) and 1 **scallion** (thinly sliced). Toss to combine, then toss with 2 small bunches **arugula** and ½ cup **walnuts**.

Turkey Roulade

No matter the celebratory occasion — Thanksgiving, New Year's, you name it — a stuffed and rolled turkey breast can fit the bill. We found it easier to butterfly and pound the bird after removing the skin, but you will absolutely want to add the skin back on before air-frying the turkey because it's key for retaining moisture (plus, it's a super-crispy snack!).

ACTIVE TIME 45 minutes   TOTAL TIME 1 hour 15 minutes   SERVES 8

4 cloves garlic, pressed

1 large shallot, finely chopped

1 cup fresh flat-leaf parsley, chopped

2 tablespoons fresh rosemary, finely chopped

1 tablespoon grated orange zest

4 tablespoons olive oil, divided

Kosher salt and pepper

2 boneless, skin-on turkey breast halves (about 1 pound each)

Fresh herbs and grapes, for topping

Prepared gravy, for topping

1. In a medium bowl, combine the garlic, shallot, parsley, rosemary, orange zest, 2 tablespoons olive oil and ½ teaspoon each salt and pepper.

2. Working with one turkey breast at a time, remove the skin in one piece, being careful not to tear it, and set aside.

3. Using a sharp knife, butterfly one of the turkey breasts, starting from the side and cutting nearly all the way through, then open like a book. Place plastic wrap over the breast and pound it to ¼ inch thick. Add the herb mixture, leaving a ¾-inch border all the way around. Starting at the short end, roll up the turkey breast. Lay the skin on top of the breast, tucking and wrapping it under edges, then tie with kitchen string, spacing about 2 inches apart. Repeat this step with the second turkey breast.

4. Brush each breast with 1 tablespoon oil and season with ¼ teaspoon salt. Heat the air fryer to 375°F. Air-fry the turkey breasts until cooked through (165°F), 20 minutes. Transfer to a cutting board and let rest at least 10 minutes.

5. Remove the string, slice and arrange on a platter. Garnish with fresh herbs and grapes. Serve with gravy.

—

PER SERVING *About 240 calories, 13.5 g fat (3 g saturated fat), 26 g protein, 300 mg sodium, 2 g carbohydrates, 1 g fiber*

TEST KITCHEN TIP

By not flipping the steak while cooking, you will achieve a better "sear" effect.

Marinated Flank Steak with Orange-Spiked Chimichurri

When you can't get to a grill, fire up the air fryer instead. We love this citrusy, herby sauce, but if you want to experiment with different marinades, simply refer to this temperature and timing for juicy steak every time.

ACTIVE TIME 15 minutes   TOTAL TIME 55 minutes   SERVES 4 to 6

FOR THE MARINATED FLANK STEAK

- 1½ tablespoons grated orange zest
- 1 tablespoon grated lime zest
- 2 tablespoons olive oil
- 1½ teaspoons cumin seeds
- 2 cloves garlic, finely chopped
- 1 1½- to 2-pound beef flank steak

  Kosher salt and pepper

FOR THE ORANGE-SPIKED CHIMICHURRI

- 1 small orange
- 1 teaspoon grated lime zest plus 1 tablespoon fresh lime juice
- 2 tablespoons olive oil
- ½ large red chile, seeded and finely chopped
- 1 scallion, finely chopped
- ½ cup fresh cilantro, chopped
- ¼ cup fresh parsley, chopped

1. In a resealable plastic bag, add the citrus zests, olive oil, cumin seeds and garlic. Add the steak, seal and turn to coat. Let sit at least 30 minutes at room temperature or refrigerate up to 2 hours.

2. Heat the air fryer to 400°F. Remove the steak from the marinade, scraping off any large bits of citrus zest, cumin seeds or garlic. Season with ½ teaspoon each salt and pepper and add to the air-fryer basket. Air-fry the steak to desired doneness, about 8 to 10 minutes for medium-rare (135°F), depending on thickness. Transfer to a cutting board and let rest 10 minutes before slicing.

3. Meanwhile, prepare the chimichurri: Using a vegetable peeler, remove 2 large strips of zest from the orange. Finely chop and place in a medium bowl. Squeeze in 2 tablespoons orange juice. Add the lime zest and juice along with the oil, chile, scallion and herbs and mix to combine. Serve the steak drizzled with the chimichurri.

—

PER SERVING *About 350 calories, 20 g fat (6 g saturated fat), 35 g protein, 310 mg sodium, 4 g carbohydrates, 1 g fiber*

With our method of brushing the meatloaf with a sauce at the end and then browning in the air fryer, you can easily sub in your favorite store-bought and homemade sauces!

Soy-Glazed Meatloaves

The secret to moist meatloaf? A generous glaze brushed over the loaf before baking. This umami-rich option is a mixture of ketchup, brown sugar and soy sauce. Add a teaspoon or two of gochujang to give this glaze a fiery kick.

ACTIVE TIME 20 minutes   TOTAL TIME 50 minutes   SERVES 6

- 2 **tablespoons ketchup**
- 1 **tablespoon brown sugar**
- 1 **tablespoon plus 1 teaspoon reduced-sodium soy sauce, divided**
- 2 **large eggs**
- 1 **tablespoon balsamic vinegar**
- **Kosher salt and pepper**
- ½ **cup panko**
- 1 **small onion, coarsely grated**
- ½ **cup fresh flat-leaf parsley, finely chopped**
- 1½ **pounds ground beef chuck**
- **Oil, for brushing (optional)**

1. Remove the insert from the air-fryer basket. Heat the air fryer to 325°F.

2. In a small bowl, combine the ketchup, brown sugar and 1 teaspoon soy sauce.

3. In a large bowl, whisk together the eggs, balsamic vinegar, remaining 1 tablespoon soy sauce and ½ teaspoon each salt and pepper; stir in the panko and let sit 2 minutes. Add the onion and parsley and mix to combine.

4. Add the beef to the panko mixture and mix until just incorporated. Shape the beef into two 7- by 4-inch loaves and place onto the air-fryer insert. (Note: If working with a stainless steel air-fryer basket, brush lightly with oil before adding meatloaves.)

5. Brush the loaves with the ketchup mixture. Return the insert (with the meatloaves) to the basket and air-fry until fully cooked (150°F), 28 to 30 minutes. Let rest at least 5 minutes before slicing.

—

PER SERVING *About 275 calories, 14.5 g fat (5.5 g saturated fat), 24 g protein, 430 mg sodium, 11 g carbohydrates, 1 g fiber*

TEST KITCHEN TIP

This salmon is also great for meal prepping! Keep it whole in the fridge, then slice right before serving. We love adding it to grain bowls along with roasted broccoli and cooked white rice.

Teriyaki Salmon

Earmark this recipe for your next dinner party! Many air fryers can fit a whole fillet of salmon. If your air fryer is on the smaller side, cut into pieces so the salmon fits in your basket and work in batches. It will still impress guests and be equally as stunning.

ACTIVE TIME 5 minutes   TOTAL TIME 25 minutes   SERVES 4

FOR THE LIME TERIYAKI SAUCE

- 1 **tablespoon mirin**
- 2 **tablespoons reduced-sodium soy sauce**
- 1 **tablespoon rice vinegar**
- 1 **tablespoon fresh lime juice**
- 1 **tablespoon dark brown sugar**

FOR THE SALMON

- 1 **1½-pound salmon fillet (cut to fit into the air-fryer basket if needed)**
- **Kosher salt**
- **Quick-Pickled Cucumbers (see below), for topping**
- **Cilantro, for topping**

1. Make the sauce: In a small bowl, combine the mirin, soy sauce, vinegar, lime juice and sugar. Set aside.

2. Make the salmon: Remove the insert from the air-fryer basket. Heat the air fryer to 400°F. Place a sheet of aluminum foil on top of the insert and place the salmon on top of that. Season with ¼ teaspoon salt. Drizzle with 2 tablespoons of the lime teriyaki sauce. Return the insert (with the salmon) to the basket and air-fry, basting every 5 minutes with any sauce that has fallen to the sides of salmon (and additional remaining sauce if necessary), until opaque throughout (125°F) and sticky on top, 15 to 18 minutes.

3. Transfer the salmon to a platter; spoon the pickled cucumbers over the top. Sprinkle with cilantro and serve with any remaining sauce.

—

PER SERVING *About 245 calories, 6 g fat (1.5 g saturated fat), 35 g protein, 675 mg sodium, 10 g carbohydrates, 0 g fiber*

Quick-Pickled Cucumbers

In a large bowl, whisk together ¼ cup **rice vinegar**, 1 teaspoon **honey** and ¼ teaspoon each **kosher salt** and **pepper** to dissolve. Stir in ½ teaspoon grated peeled fresh **ginger** and 1 **shallot** (thinly sliced); let sit 5 minutes. Toss with 2 **Persian cucumbers** (thinly sliced) and let sit, tossing occasionally, 10 minutes. Drain.

Striped Bass with Radish Salsa Verde

The star of this fish dish is the herb-packed salsa-like topping featuring peppery radishes plus their leafy tops, as well as a few other flavor-packed ingredients. To enjoy the salsa with another protein, simply prepare it with a drizzle of olive oil, salt and pepper and check out our Quick Cooking Guide.

ACTIVE TIME 35 minutes   TOTAL TIME 40 minutes   SERVES 4

- 1 clove garlic, pressed
- 1 tablespoon anchovy paste, or 3 anchovy fillets, finely chopped
- ½ small red onion, finely chopped
- 1 tablespoon red wine vinegar
- ½ cup plus 1 tablespoon olive oil, divided
- 1 bunch radishes, diced, leaves separated and finely chopped
- 1 cup fresh flat-leaf parsley, finely chopped
- 1 teaspoon fresh tarragon, finely chopped
- 4 6-ounce striped bass fillets
- Kosher salt and pepper

1. In a medium bowl, combine the garlic, anchovy paste, onion and vinegar and let sit 5 minutes.

2. Stir in ½ cup oil, then the radishes and greens, parsley and tarragon.

3. Heat the air fryer to 400°F. Pat the fish dry, then brush with the remaining 1 tablespoon oil and season with ½ teaspoon each salt and pepper. Add to the air-fryer basket, skin side down, and air-fry until the skin is crispy and the fish is opaque throughout (125°F), 8 to 10 minutes. Serve topped with the radish salsa verde.

—

PER SERVING *About 465 calories, 35.5 g fat (5 g saturated fat), 33 g protein, 640 mg sodium, 3 g carbohydrates, 1 g fiber*

make it a meal

Serve the fillets with your go-to grain (we suggest quinoa or farro). Or turn them into fish tacos: Use your air fryer to quickly warm tortillas, then slice the fillets and add to tortillas before topping with the radish salsa verde. Add a spoonful of sour cream or Greek yogurt if desired.

TEST KITCHEN TIP
Our recipe calls for more cornstarch than you'll need to evenly coat the tofu — similar to how you use extra flour for dredging chicken cutlets — so you'll end up throwing some away. We tried using a smaller quantity and found that the cornstarch clumped up.

Crispy Tofu with Peanut Sauce

Thanks to the circulating hot air and a cornstarch dredge, it's easier than ever to get crispy tofu — no pressing required! Feel free to sub in gluten-free tamari for the soy sauce.

ACTIVE TIME 25 minutes TOTAL TIME 45 minutes, plus marinating SERVES 4

FOR THE TOFU

- 2 12.3-ounce packages extra-firm tofu
- 1 tablespoon reduced-sodium soy sauce or tamari
- 3 tablespoons canola oil
- 1 teaspoon grated garlic
- 2/3 cup cornstarch

FOR THE PEANUT TAMARI SAUCE

- 3 tablespoons natural smooth peanut butter
- 1 1/2 tablespoons reduced-sodium soy sauce or tamari
- 1 tablespoon agave or honey
- 1 tablespoon fresh lime juice
- 1/4 cup hot water
- 1 teaspoon grated garlic
- 1/4 teaspoon grated peeled fresh ginger
- 1 teaspoon sriracha
- 1 tablespoon toasted sesame oil

  Sliced scallions and Fresno chiles, chopped cilantro and roasted peanuts, for topping

1. Make the tofu: Remove the tofu from the packaging, pat dry with paper towels and cut into 3/4-inch cubes.

2. In a small bowl, whisk together the soy sauce and canola oil, then stir in the garlic. Pour 1/3 of the marinade into a 9- by 13-inch or shallow baking dish, coating the bottom evenly. Add the tofu cubes to the dish. Pour the remaining marinade on top and gently turn the cubes to coat; let marinate at room temperature for 45 minutes.

3. Make the sauce: In a medium bowl, combine the peanut butter, soy sauce, agave and lime juice. Gradually whisk in the hot water to emulsify. Whisk in the garlic, ginger, sriracha and sesame oil. Set aside.

4. Heat the air fryer to 400°F. Place the cornstarch in a shallow bowl. Carefully dredge the marinated tofu cubes in the cornstarch, coating evenly and shaking off any excess. Working in batches if needed, add the cubes to the air-fryer basket, leaving space so they are not touching. Air-fry, shaking the basket twice, until golden brown and crisp, 15 to 18 minutes.

5. Drizzle the tofu with the sauce and serve topped with the scallions, chiles, cilantro and peanuts

—

PER SERVING *About 480 calories, 29 g fat (3 g saturated fat), 21 g protein, 410 mg sodium, 32 g carbohydrates, 3 g fiber*

TEST KITCHEN TIP

Can't imagine pizza
without sauce?
We successfully
tested spreading
some onto the dough
before adding the
cheese and meat.

Pepperoni Pizza

Yes, you can even make pizza! Give the dough a head start in the air fryer before adding any toppings to ensure that it gets fully cooked and other elements don't burn. Using parchment paper leads to a soggier crust, so instead, shape the dough directly in the air-fryer basket. To avoid a mess of melted cheese, go for sliced provolone rather than traditional shredded mozzarella.

ACTIVE TIME 15 minutes   TOTAL TIME 45 minutes   SERVES 4

1 small red onion, thinly sliced into half-moons

2 tablespoons olive oil, plus more for brushing

Kosher salt

4 ounces sliced pepperoni

12 pepperoncini, thinly sliced

All-purpose flour, for dusting

1 pound pizza dough, halved

8 slices provolone cheese

Honey, for drizzling

1. In a small bowl, toss the onion with 2 tablespoons olive oil and ¼ teaspoon salt. Add the pepperoni and pepperoncini and toss to combine.

2. On a lightly floured surface, shape each piece of dough to the size of the insert in the bottom of the air-fryer basket.

3. Remove the air-fryer insert and brush with oil. Place one piece of pizza dough on top and return the insert to the basket. Return the basket to the air fryer and heat the air fryer to 400°F (the pizza dough will begin to cook as it heats). Once the air fryer reaches 400°F, air-fry 3 minutes. Using tongs, flip and air-fry 2 minutes more.

4. Top the pizza with 4 slices of provolone and half of the pepperoni mixture. Air-fry until the crust is golden brown and crisp, 7 to 8 minutes more.

5. Transfer to a cutting board and drizzle with honey. Repeat with the remaining dough, cheese and toppings.

—

PER SERVING *About 710 calories, 39 g fat (16 g saturated fat), 26 g protein, 2,265 mg sodium, 59 g carbohydrates, 2 g fiber*

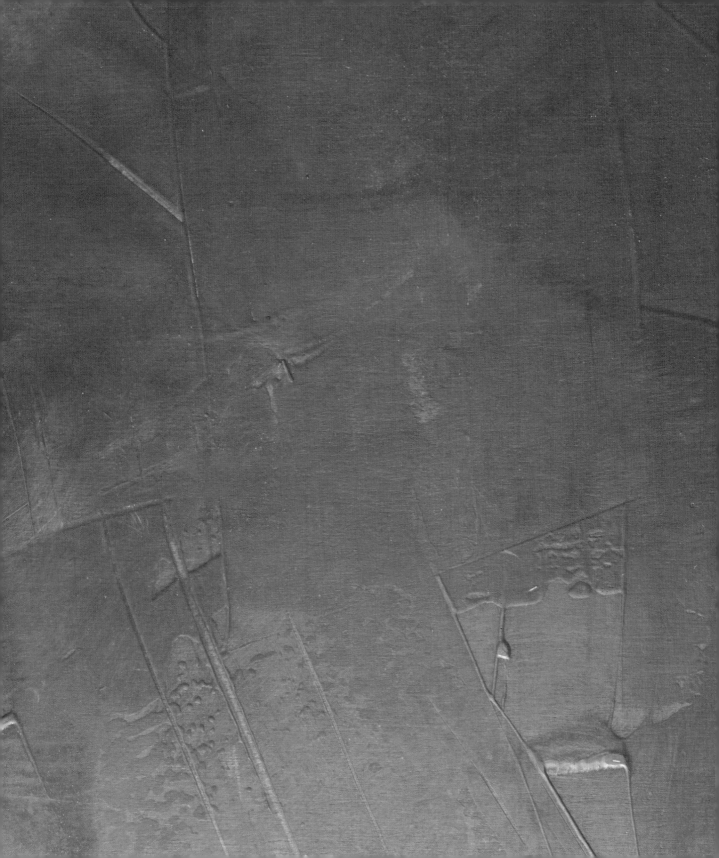

chapter four

Sides

Free up some oven space! Whether you want to roast vegetables until caramelized or replicate the charred notes you would get from firing up the grill, air fryers can help you. Hit the farmers' market and select a recipe based on what's in season — or skip straight ahead to the cheesy garlic bread.

RECIPES

Roasted Asparagus with Creamy Feta

A quick stint in a superhot air fryer helps you cook asparagus without losing crispness and spares you from having to deal with parboiling and setting up an ice bath. Serve this spring vegetable on top of a creamy feta blend or skip steps 3 and 4 and simply enjoy.

ACTIVE TIME 15 minutes   TOTAL TIME 15 minutes   SERVES 3 or 4

1 pound asparagus, trimmed

1 tablespoon olive oil

Kosher salt and pepper

4 ounces feta cheese

¼ cup plain whole milk yogurt

1 lemon

1. In a large bowl, toss the asparagus with the oil and ¼ teaspoon each salt and pepper.

2. Heat the air fryer to 400°F. Add the asparagus to the air-fryer basket and air-fry, shaking the basket halfway through, 10 minutes.

3. Meanwhile, in a food processor, puree the feta and yogurt until smooth. Spread half of the mixture onto a platter.

4. Grate the zest from half of the lemon over the cooked asparagus. Using tongs, quickly toss to combine, then arrange the asparagus on top of the feta mixture.

—

PER SERVING *About 170 calories, 13.5 g fat (6.5 g saturated fat), 8 g protein, 525 mg sodium, 6 g carbohydrates, 2 g fiber*

switch it up

Skip serving the stalks on a bed of creamy dressing and try tossing them in a vinaigrette instead! In a small bowl, combine 1 tablespoon **rice vinegar**, 1 small **shallot** (finely chopped) and ¼ teaspoon each **kosher salt** and **pepper**. Let sit while the asparagus is in the air fryer. Stir in 1 tablespoon **olive oil**, then gently toss with ¼ cup fresh **mint** (chopped) and 2 ounces **feta** (crumbled). Spoon over asparagus and sprinkle with 2 tablespoons fresh **dill** (roughly chopped).

TEST KITCHEN TIP
Prefer fresh artichokes? You'll need to adjust the cooking time. (If halves aren't golden brown after 12 minutes, give them a little longer.)

Parmesan-Thyme Artichokes

Grab canned artichokes from the pantry and you'll have a crispy, cheesy accompaniment in no time. Take note: It is super important to pat the artichoke hearts dry, otherwise you'll wind up with a soggy side (and who wants that?!).

ACTIVE TIME 10 minutes   TOTAL TIME 20 minutes   SERVES 4

2   tablespoons olive oil

2   cloves garlic, grated

2   teaspoons fresh thyme

   Kosher salt and pepper

2   14-ounce cans artichoke hearts, halved and patted very dry

1/3   cup grated Parmesan cheese, divided

1/2   lemon

2   tablespoons fresh flat-leaf parsley, chopped

1. Heat the air fryer to 400°F. In a large bowl, combine the oil, garlic, thyme, 1/4 teaspoon salt and 1/2 teaspoon pepper. Add the artichokes and gently toss to coat, then gently toss with 3 tablespoons Parmesan.

2. Add the artichokes to the air-fryer basket, cut sides up, and top with the remaining 2 tablespoons Parmesan. Air-fry, shaking the basket halfway through, until golden brown and crisp around the edges, 10 to 12 minutes.

3. Transfer to a platter, then grate the zest of the lemon half on top and sprinkle with parsley.

—

PER SERVING *About 145 calories, 8.5 g fat (2 g saturated fat), 5 g protein, 635 mg sodium, 11 g carbohydrates, 2 g fiber*

make it a meal

While this cheesy side tastes great served with seared chicken or lemony pork tenderloin, it can also be the star of a charcuterie-inspired, board-style dinner. Set the artichokes out on a platter with sliced cucumbers, olives, roasted red peppers, tomatoes, crusty bread or crackers and your favorite meats and cheeses.

TEST KITCHEN TIP

To ensure a softer texture on the inside, start by soaking the plantains in water, which prevents them from drying out during the frying process.

Tostones

Crispy flattened green plantains are typically prepared by frying slices, then smashing or pressing them and frying again. We replicated this twice-fried process using the air fryer.

ACTIVE TIME 25 minutes   TOTAL TIME 45 minutes   SERVES 4

FOR THE TOSTONES

3	green plantains
2	tablespoons fresh lime juice
	Kosher salt
3	tablespoons canola oil, divided
¼	teaspoon smoked paprika

FOR THE SAUCE

1½	cups fresh cilantro
½	ripe Hass avocado
½	serrano chile, chopped
1	clove garlic
1	scallion, green part only, roughly chopped
2	tablespoons fresh lime juice
1	tablespoon white vinegar
¼	teaspoon agave or honey
	Kosher salt

1. Make the tostones: Peel and cut the plantains into ¾-inch-thick slices.

2. In a large bowl, stir together the lime juice, 2 teaspoons salt and 4 cups water until the salt dissolves. Add the plantains and let soak 20 minutes.

3. Meanwhile, make the sauce: In a blender, puree the ingredients until smooth, adjusting consistency with ¼ to ½ cup water as needed; season with salt. Pour sauce in a bowl and press a piece of parchment paper or plastic wrap directly onto the surface of the sauce and refrigerate until ready to serve.

4. Heat the air fryer to 350°F. Drain the plantains but do not dry (a little excess water helps to soften them). In a large bowl, toss the plantains with 1 tablespoon oil. Add to the air-fryer basket, spacing them about ½ inch apart, and air-fry 5 minutes. Using tongs, flip and air-fry 4 minutes more.

5. Transfer the tostones to a piece of parchment on a work surface. Working quickly and using a heavy glass or mug, smash each one to about ¼ inch thick (clean the bottom of the glass occasionally to prevent sticking). If the tostones cool and harden, reheat briefly in the air fryer to more easily smash.

6. Heat the air fryer to 400°F. Brush both sides of half the tostones with 1 tablespoon oil and sprinkle with ¼ teaspoon salt. Add to the basket, spacing them about ½ inch apart, and air-fry until the edges start to turn light golden brown, 3 to 4 minutes. Using tongs, flip and air-fry until crisp and golden brown around the edges, 4 minutes more. Transfer to a platter.

7. Repeat step 6 with the remaining tostones, 1 tablespoon of oil and ¼ teaspoon salt. When the second batch is ready, top with the first batch and air-fry until reheated and crisp, 1 to 2 minutes more. Transfer tostones to the platter, sprinkle with the paprika and serve immediately with the sauce.

—

PER SERVING *About 300 calories, 14.5 g fat (1.5 g saturated fat), 2 g protein, 370 mg sodium, 64 g carbohydrates, 6 g fiber*

Crispy Potatoes with Bacon

If you've ever fried an egg in leftover bacon grease, you know the delicious powers it holds. Here, small spuds start cooking under slices of bacon, which saves time and infuses more flavor as the potatoes absorb some of the bacon grease. Toss it all with a tangy mustard vinaigrette before serving to brighten it up.

ACTIVE TIME 15 minutes   TOTAL TIME 30 minutes   SERVES 4

1 ½ **pounds small new potatoes (about 32), halved**

4 **sprigs thyme, plus 1 teaspoon thyme leaves**

1 **tablespoon olive oil**

Kosher salt and pepper

3 **slices bacon**

3 **medium shallots, cut into ¼-inch wedges**

1 **tablespoon white or regular balsamic vinegar**

2 **teaspoons whole-grain mustard**

1. Heat the air fryer to 400°F. In a large bowl, toss the potatoes and thyme sprigs with the oil, ½ teaspoon salt and ¼ teaspoon pepper. Add to the air-fryer basket and top with the bacon. Air-fry until the bacon is crisp, 6 to 12 minutes. Transfer the bacon to a paper-towel-lined plate and let cool before breaking into pieces.

2. Shake the potatoes and continue to air-fry, 8 minutes. Add the shallots to the basket with the potatoes, toss to combine and air-fry until the vegetables are golden brown and tender, 8 to 12 minutes more.

3. Meanwhile, in a large bowl, whisk together the vinegar, mustard and thyme leaves. Transfer the cooked vegetables to the bowl, adding any oils from the bottom of the basket, and toss to combine. Fold in the bacon and serve.

—

PER SERVING *About 275 calories, 11.5 g fat (3.5 g saturated fat), 7 g protein, 430 mg sodium, 35 g carbohydrates, 3 g fiber*

love your leftovers

Any extra spuds will continue to absorb more flavor as they sit in your fridge in an airtight container. (Yum!) Turn them into a quick breakfast hash to enjoy the next morning: Chop everything and reheat in a skillet or the air fryer until crisp. Serve topped with a fried egg.

Blistered Snap Peas

Crank up the heat to give this crisp springtime delight a beautiful char, similar to what you could achieve on an outdoor grill. For an extra hit of deliciousness, season the sweet peas with gochugaru, a vibrant red Korean chile powder.

ACTIVE TIME 10 minutes   TOTAL TIME 15 minutes   SERVES 4

1 pound snap peas, strings removed

2 tablespoons olive oil

½ to 1 teaspoon gochugaru

Kosher salt

½ lemon, plus wedges for serving

Fresh cilantro, chopped, for topping

1. Heat the air fryer to 400°F. In a large bowl, toss the snap peas with the oil, gochugaru and ½ teaspoon salt.

2. Add the snap peas to the air-fryer basket and air-fry until slightly charred and just tender, 5 to 6 minutes.

3. Squeeze the juice of the lemon half on top. Using tongs, quickly toss to combine, then transfer the snap peas to a shallow bowl or platter. Serve with lemon wedges and sprinkle with cilantro.

—

PER SERVING *About 110 calories, 7 g fat (1 g saturated fat), 4 g protein, 245 mg sodium, 10 g carbohydrates, 3 g fiber*

2 tablespoons olive oil

1 tablespoon red wine vinegar

1 tablespoon tomato paste

2 teaspoons garam masala

1 teaspoon honey

⅛ teaspoon cayenne

Kosher salt

1 medium head cauliflower (about 2 pounds), cut into florets

6 cloves garlic, smashed

1 onion, cut into ½-inch-thick wedges (root end intact)

½ pound green beans, trimmed and halved

Chopped fresh cilantro, for topping

1. Heat the air fryer to 370°F. In a large bowl, whisk together the oil, vinegar, tomato paste, garam masala, honey, cayenne and ½ teaspoon salt.

2. Add the cauliflower and toss to coat. Add the garlic and onion and toss. Transfer to the air-fryer basket and air-fry until beginning to roast, 8 minutes.

3. Add the green beans to the basket and toss to combine. Continue air-frying until the vegetables are tender and roasted, 5 minutes more. Transfer to a platter, then sprinkle with cilantro.

—

PER SERVING *About 315 calories, 7.5 g fat (1 g saturated fat), 7 g protein, 390 mg sodium, 55 g carbohydrates, 5 g fiber*

Spice-Roasted Cauliflower and Green Beans

This sweet-savory roasted vegetable dish is a superstar. Pay attention to the timing when you're dealing with ingredients of different sizes (and densities!), cooking in stages if needed to make sure each element sings. The cauliflower florets are a bit sturdier, so we put them in the air fryer first and held off on adding the green beans until much later because those crisp up relatively quickly.

ACTIVE TIME 15 minutes   TOTAL TIME 45 minutes   SERVES 4

Broccolini and Mushrooms with Salsa Macha

Salsa macha — made from dried chiles, nuts and oil — adds smoky and spicy notes to any dish. Charred Broccolini especially benefits from a drizzle of this condiment, and when presented on a bed of creamy, cooling ricotta, this side is perfectly balanced.

ACTIVE TIME 5 minutes   TOTAL TIME 20 minutes   SERVES 4

10 ounces oyster mushrooms, separated

2 tablespoons olive oil, divided

Kosher salt and pepper

2 bunches Broccolini, trimmed and cut into large florets

1 cup ricotta cheese

1 teaspoon grated lemon zest

Milk, as needed

3 tablespoons store-bought salsa macha

1. Heat the air fryer to 400°F. In a large bowl, toss the mushrooms with 1 tablespoon oil and a pinch each of salt and pepper.

2. Add the mushrooms to the air-fryer basket and air-fry 5 minutes; shake the basket and air-fry 3 minutes more.

3. In the same large bowl, toss the Broccolini with the remaining tablespoon oil and ¼ teaspoon each salt and pepper. Add to the basket (with the mushrooms) and air-fry until just tender, 5 minutes.

4. Meanwhile, in a medium bowl, mix the ricotta and lemon zest, adding enough milk so the mixture is smooth. Spread onto a large plate or platter.

5. Arrange the Broccolini and mushrooms on top of the ricotta spread. Spoon the salsa macha on top.

—

PER SERVING *About 285 calories, 16 g fat (9 g saturated fat), 13 g protein, 400 mg sodium, 12 g carbohydrates, 6 g fiber*

make it a meal

Pair this with a grilled steak or pile everything on top of cooked pizza dough or thick slices of toasted country bread.

TEST KITCHEN TIP

Skip the butter and spread one of these condiments on your corn instead: harissa, garlic-herb cheese spread, pimiento cheese or pesto.

Corn on the Cob

Savor sweet, juicy corn without having to turn on the grill or stove. Test out our foolproof strategy for cooking up corn (note: the time stays the same whether you're making one or four ears). Then mix it up with all the toppings, from store-bought condiments to homemade flavored butters.

ACTIVE TIME 5 minutes   **TOTAL TIME** 25 minutes   **SERVES** 4

4 **ears corn, partially shucked**

Paprika, sour cream and chives, for topping

1. Trim the corn if needed to fit into the air-fryer basket. Heat the air fryer to 400°F.

2. Add the corn to the basket and air-fry 10 minutes. Using tongs, flip and air-fry until tender, 10 minutes more. Peel down the remaining husks and serve with desired toppings, like a flavored butter (below) or paprika, sour cream and chives.

—

PER SERVING *About 90 calories, 1 g fat (0 g saturated fat), 3 g protein, 15 mg sodium, 19 g carbohydrates, 2 g fiber*

Boosted Butters

Up the fun and spread each cob with flavored butter. For each, mix the ingredients in a medium bowl to combine, then, using plastic wrap, shape the mixture into a log and twist the ends to seal; refrigerate for up to 2 weeks or freeze for up to 2 months.

MISO GARLIC
½ cup (1 stick) unsalted butter (at room temperature) + 2 tablespoons red miso paste + 1 small clove garlic (grated) + 1 scallion (finely chopped) + 1 tablespoon toasted sesame seeds

SMOKY CHEDDAR
½ cup (1 stick) unsalted butter (at room temperature) + 1 ounce extra-sharp Cheddar cheese (grated) + ¼ teaspoon smoked paprika + 1 tablespoon fresh cilantro (finely chopped) + 1 teaspoon lime zest + 2 teaspoons fresh lime juice

HERBY MUSTARD
½ cup (1 stick) unsalted butter (at room temperature) + ½ small shallot (finely chopped; about 2 tablespoons) + 1 tablespoon fresh flat-leaf parsley (chopped) + 1 to 2 teaspoons Dijon mustard + 1 teaspoon fresh thyme

HOT HONEY
½ cup (1 stick) unsalted butter (at room temperature) + 1 tablespoon habanero hot sauce (plus more to taste) + 2 teaspoons honey + 1 tablespoon fresh chives (chopped)

TEST KITCHEN TIP

Cut the vegetable you're throwing into the air fryer (here, carrots) into evenly sized pieces, so everything cooks at a similar speed.

Roasted Carrots and Chickpeas with Marinated Feta

This combination of caramelized carrots, extra-crunchy chickpeas and briny marinated feta will wow when served alongside any main (imagine grilled chicken or roasted pork tenderloin). Giving the canned chickpeas a head start in the air fryer ensures that they crisp up without overcooking the seasoned carrots.

ACTIVE TIME 20 minutes   TOTAL TIME 45 minutes   SERVES 6

1   **15.5-ounce can chickpeas, drained, rinsed and patted dry**

5   **tablespoons olive oil, divided**

1   **teaspoon cumin seeds, divided**

   Kosher salt and pepper

1   **pound carrots, trimmed, scrubbed and halved lengthwise if large**

1   **small shallot, thinly sliced**

1   **Fresno chile, thinly sliced**

1   **tablespoon red wine vinegar**

4   **ounces feta cheese, drained, patted dry and cut into pieces**

1   **tablespoon fresh oregano, roughly chopped**

1   **tablespoon fresh mint, roughly chopped**

1. In a large bowl, toss the chickpeas with 1 tablespoon oil, ½ teaspoon cumin seeds and ¼ teaspoon each salt and pepper.

2. Heat the air fryer to 400°F. Add the chickpeas to the air-fryer basket and air-fry, shaking halfway through, 10 minutes.

3. Meanwhile, in the same large bowl, toss the carrots with 1 tablespoon oil, the remaining ½ teaspoon cumin seeds and ¼ teaspoon each salt and pepper.

4. Add the carrots to the basket (with the chickpeas) and air-fry until the carrots are golden brown and tender and the chickpeas are crispy, 15 to 17 minutes.

5. Meanwhile, in a medium bowl, combine the shallot, chile, vinegar and ¼ teaspoon salt. Stir in the remaining 3 tablespoons oil, then gently fold in the feta and herbs.

6. Transfer the carrots and chickpeas to a platter and spoon the marinated feta on top.

—

PER SERVING *About 465 calories, 17 g fat (4.5 g saturated fat), 7 g protein, 555 mg sodium, 19 g carbohydrates, 7 g fiber*

Cheesy Garlic Bread

Thanks to a homemade compound butter and two types of cheese, you will get to enjoy cheesy, garlicky goodness in every single bite. Plus, our secret ingredients — a sprinkle of lemon zest and a spoonful of Dijon — add just enough brightness and acidity to balance the richness of the cheese and butter. Yum!

ACTIVE TIME 15 minutes   TOTAL TIME 35 minutes   SERVES 4 to 6

½ cup (1 stick) unsalted butter, at room temperature

2 cloves garlic, finely grated

1 teaspoon grated lemon zest

½ teaspoon Dijon mustard

   Kosher salt and pepper

¼ cup fresh flat-leaf parsley, finely chopped

2 tablespoons grated Parmesan cheese

2 tablespoons grated pecorino cheese

4 hero-size rolls, split

1. In a medium bowl, combine the butter, garlic, lemon zest, Dijon and ¼ teaspoon each salt and pepper. Fold in the parsley, Parmesan and pecorino.

2. Heat the air fryer to 350°F. Add 4 sliced roll halves to the air-fryer basket and air-fry 2 minutes. Remove and spread the compound butter to cover each half. Return to the basket and air-fry until golden brown and crispy, 5 minutes more. Transfer to a cutting board. Repeat with the remaining roll halves. Slice the garlic bread before serving.

—

PER SERVING *About 350 calories, 25 g fat (14 g saturated fat), 2 g protein, 400 mg sodium, 29 g carbohydrates, 3 g fiber*

meal prep magic

Before air-frying, wrap garlic bread in aluminum foil and store in an airtight container in the freezer for up to 6 months. When ready to eat, proceed with air-frying instructions, adding an additional few minutes as needed.

Sweet and Spicy Brussels Sprouts

Take Brussels sprouts to new heights with a maple-sriracha glaze that offers just the right amount of sweet heat. Seasoning the sprouts twice is key — once before roasting in the air fryer, then tossing them with the sauce after they're charred and crispy.

ACTIVE TIME 10 minutes   TOTAL TIME 30 minutes   SERVES 8

2 pounds Brussels sprouts, trimmed and halved

5 tablespoons olive oil, divided

1/2 teaspoon hot paprika

Kosher salt

6 tablespoons pure maple syrup

1 1/2 tablespoons sriracha

Aleppo pepper and sliced scallions, for topping

1. Heat the air fryer to 375°F. In a large bowl, toss the Brussels sprouts with 4 tablespoons oil. Add the paprika and 1/2 teaspoon salt and toss to coat. Working in batches if needed, add the sprouts to the air-fryer basket and air-fry until charred, crispy and tender, 9 to 11 minutes.

2. Meanwhile, in a large bowl, whisk together the maple syrup, sriracha and a pinch of salt. Transfer 2 1/2 tablespoons of the sauce to a small bowl and whisk in the remaining tablespoon oil; set aside for serving.

3. Transfer the roasted Brussels sprouts to the large bowl with the maple-sriracha sauce and toss to fully coat. (If you roasted in batches, add each batch to the bowl as it finishes, tossing well after adding the final batch to ensure all the sprouts are fully coated with the sauce.)

4. Transfer to a platter, then drizzle with the reserved sauce mixture and sprinkle with Aleppo pepper and scallions.

—

PER SERVING *About 160 calories, 9 g fat (1 g saturated fat), 3 g protein, 220 mg sodium, 20 g carbohydrates, 4 g fiber*

switch it up

Instead of coating the Brussels sprouts with the maple-sriracha sauce and topping with Aleppo pepper and scallions, sprinkle air-fried sprouts with lemon zest and sea salt or toss with pepitas and dried mission figs.

TEST KITCHEN TIP
By making small slits in each spud (a.k.a. "hasselbacking"), you seriously cut down on the cooking time.

Hasselback Potatoes

Hasselback Potatoes

Accordion baked taters have extra nooks for butter, making them a total game changer. They also cook in a fraction of the time of classic baked spuds. Win-win.

ACTIVE TIME 10 minutes TOTAL TIME 40 minutes SERVES 4

- 4 medium yellow potatoes (about 7 ounces each)
- 2 tablespoons olive oil

   Flaky sea salt and pepper

- 6 tablespoons unsalted butter, at room temperature
- 2 scallions, finely chopped

1. Heat the air fryer to 400°F. With a sharp knife, make vertical slits in the potatoes, ⅛ to ¼ inch apart, being sure to stop at least ¼ inch before the bottom (do not cut all the way through).

2. Rub the potatoes with the oil and ½ teaspoon each flaky sea salt and pepper. Transfer to the basket, cut sides up. Air-fry until tender, golden brown and crisp, about 30 minutes.

3. Meanwhile, in a small bowl, combine the butter and scallions. Dollop each potato with scallion butter and serve.

—

PER SERVING *About 380 calories, 24 g fat (11.5 g saturated fat), 5 g protein, 595 mg sodium, 36 g carbohydrates, 3 g fiber*

Roasted Kale and Mushrooms

For even cooking, this recipe air-fries everything in stages.

ACTIVE TIME 20 minutes TOTAL TIME 25 minutes SERVES 5

- 4 small shallots (about 3 ounces), peeled and halved
- 6 tablespoons olive oil, divided

   Kosher salt and pepper

- 6 ounces oyster mushrooms, separated
- 1 large bunch green curly kale (12 ounces), ribs removed, leaves torn into large pieces

1. Heat the air fryer to 400°F. In a large bowl, toss the shallots with 1 tablespoon oil and a pinch each of salt and pepper.

2. Add the shallots to the air-fryer basket and air-fry 5 minutes. Using tongs, flip the shallots and air-fry 5 minutes more.

3. In the same large bowl, toss the mushrooms with 2 tablespoons oil and ¼ teaspoon each salt and pepper. Add the mushrooms to the basket (with the shallots) and air-fry 5 minutes more.

4. In the same large bowl, toss the kale with the remaining 3 tablespoons oil and ¼ teaspoon each salt and pepper. Push the mushrooms and shallots to one side of the basket and add the kale to the other side. Air-fry until the kale has wilted and has slightly crispy edges, 3 minutes. Toss together and transfer to a platter.

—

PER SERVING *About 195 calories, 17 g fat (2 g saturated fat), 4 g protein, 250 mg sodium, 10 g carbohydrates, 4 g fiber*

TEST KITCHEN TIP

Masa harina — popularly used to make tortillas and tamales — is a flour made from finely ground hominy, or dried corn kernels that have been soaked in limewater (an alkalized solution).

Cheesy Seasoned Zucchini

Sprinkle a combination of cotija cheese, masa harina and spices over zucchini slices to take the summer vegetable from basic to beyond delicious. The masa harina adds a toasted corn flavor, which rounds out the dish, plus it gives everything an interesting texture (and zucchini can definitely benefit from a bit of unexpected crunch!).

ACTIVE TIME 10 minutes   TOTAL TIME 35 minutes   SERVES 4

2 tablespoons olive oil, plus more for brushing

2 teaspoons grated garlic

3 medium-small zucchini (about 1 ¼ pounds), cut into ⅓-inch-thick rings

3 tablespoons masa harina

⅛ teaspoon cayenne

¼ cup plus 1 tablespoon grated cotija cheese, divided

1 ¼ teaspoons ground cumin, divided

Kosher salt

½ teaspoon Tajín seasoning

2 tablespoons fresh cilantro, chopped

1. In a large bowl, combine the oil and garlic. Add the zucchini and toss to coat.

2. In a small bowl, combine the masa, cayenne, ¼ cup cotija, 1 teaspoon cumin and ½ teaspoon salt. Sprinkle over the zucchini and toss to coat.

3. Heat the air fryer to 400°F. Brush the air-fryer basket with oil and add half of the zucchini, separating the pieces so there is as much space as possible (there will be some overlapping). Air-fry until tender and topping is golden brown, 12 to 14 minutes. Repeat with the remaining zucchini.

4. Transfer the zucchini to a platter and sprinkle with the Tajín, remaining tablespoon cotija, ¼ teaspoon cumin and the cilantro.
—

PER SERVING *About 155 calories, 12 g fat (2 g saturated fat), 4 g protein, 475 mg sodium, 10 g carbohydrates, 2 g fiber*

love your leftovers

Turn extra zucchini slices into "chips" to dip in salsa. Cool completely, then store in an airtight container in the fridge. Reheat in the air fryer until nice and crispy.

chapter five

All-in-One Dinners

With the right strategy, you can cook up a complete meal in the air fryer in 45 minutes or less — from crispy cauliflower tacos to sizzling steak fajitas, spicy shrimp lettuce wraps and cheesy meatball subs. Fewer dirty dishes? Count us in!

RECIPES

TEST KITCHEN TIP

Set up a DIY potato bar! Skip step 4, leaving the black bean topping in a bowl. Other topping ideas: salsa, barbecue sauce, pickles, even bacon (see page 35).

Poblano and Black Bean Loaded Potatoes

With melted cheese, smoky beans and starchy spuds, this budget-friendly vegetarian dinner is pure comfort. If you're short on time, you can nuke the potatoes in the microwave on High for 10 minutes to soften, then just throw them in the air fryer to crisp up for a few minutes before adding the cheese.

ACTIVE TIME 20 minutes TOTAL TIME 45 minutes SERVES 4

4   medium russet potatoes (about 8 ounces each), scrubbed and dried

4 1/2   teaspoons olive oil, divided

Kosher salt

2   poblano peppers, chopped

1/2   15-ounce can black beans, drained and rinsed (about 3/4 cup)

1/4   teaspoon ground cumin

1/8   teaspoon smoked paprika

1   large plum tomato, seeded and chopped

1/2   teaspoon grated lime zest, plus more for topping, plus 2 teaspoons fresh lime juice

1/3   cup sour cream

Grated Cheddar cheese, for topping (optional)

1. Heat the air fryer to 400°F. Prick the potatoes all over with a fork, then brush with 1 tablespoon oil and sprinkle with 1/4 teaspoon salt. Place the potatoes in the air-fryer basket and air-fry 20 minutes. Using tongs, flip and air-fry until tender, 15 to 20 minutes more.

2. Meanwhile, in a small bowl, toss the poblanos with 1 teaspoon oil and 1/4 teaspoon salt. In a second small bowl, toss the beans with the cumin, paprika, 1/4 teaspoon salt and remaining 1/2 teaspoon oil. In a third small bowl, toss the tomato with the lime juice and a pinch of salt. In a fourth small bowl, combine the sour cream and lime zest.

3. Remove the potatoes from the basket and transfer to a plate. Add the poblanos to the basket in a single layer and air-fry until tender, 5 to 6 minutes. Transfer to the bowl with the black beans and fold to combine.

4. Split the potatoes, top with cheese (if using), then top with the bean-poblano mixture. Return the potatoes to the basket and air-fry just until the cheese melts and the bean mixture is warmed through, 1 to 2 minutes. Serve topped with the tomato, sour cream and more lime zest.

—

PER SERVING *About 430 calories, 11 g fat (3 g saturated fat), 15 g protein, 540 mg sodium, 71 g carbohydrates, 13 g fiber*

Falafel Salad

For faster falafel, start with canned chickpeas (instead of soaking dried ones) and quickly pulse in a food processor along with spices and seasonings. Round out the Mediterranean meal with a light and bright salad featuring marinated cucumbers and fresh mint.

ACTIVE TIME 15 minutes   TOTAL TIME 35 minutes   SERVES 4

- 2 cloves garlic
- 4 scallions, white and green parts thinly sliced separately
- 6 ½ cups baby kale, divided
- 2 15-ounce cans chickpeas, drained and rinsed
- 1 teaspoon grated lemon zest plus 2 tablespoons fresh lemon juice
- 2 tablespoons all-purpose flour
- 1 teaspoon ground cumin
- 1 teaspoon ground coriander
- Kosher salt
- 3 tablespoons olive oil, divided, plus more for brushing
- ½ English cucumber, thinly sliced on the bias
- ½ cup fresh parsley
- ¼ cup fresh mint
- Greek yogurt, for topping

1. In a food processor, pulse the garlic, scallion whites and ½ cup baby kale until very finely chopped. Add the chickpeas, lemon zest, flour, cumin, coriander and ½ teaspoon salt and pulse to combine (the chickpeas should be chopped but coarse). Form the mixture into 24 balls (about 2 tablespoons each).

2. Heat the air fryer to 325°F. Brush the basket with oil and add half of the falafel. Air-fry 15 minutes. Brush the falafel with ½ tablespoon oil and increase the air fryer temperature to 400°F. Air-fry until deeply golden brown, 4 minutes more. Transfer to a plate. Repeat with the remaining falafel and ½ tablespoon oil.

3. In a large bowl, whisk together the lemon juice and remaining 2 tablespoons oil. Add the cucumber and marinate 5 minutes. Add the remaining 6 cups baby kale, parsley, mint, scallion greens and ½ teaspoon salt and toss. Top with the falafel and a dollop of yogurt.

—

PER SERVING *About 345calories, 16 g fat (2.5 g saturated fat), 14 g protein, 805 mg sodium, 40 g carbohydrates, 12 g fiber*

make it ahead

Freeze uncooked falafel balls on a baking sheet until firm. Transfer to a container and keep in the freezer for up to 2 months. To enjoy, air-fry from frozen, adding extra time as needed.

Crispy Cauliflower Tacos

Tacos make a fantastic all-in-one dinner because you can choose a single component to cook (here, we're crisping up spiced cauliflower) and then prep the rest of your fresh ingredients while the air fryer does its thing. A colorful, crunchy slaw takes just a few more minutes to toss together, but in a pinch, you can top with shredded carrots or cabbage and a squeeze of lime.

ACTIVE TIME 10 minutes   TOTAL TIME 25 minutes   SERVES 4

- 2 tablespoons olive oil
- 1 tablespoon fresh lime juice, plus lime wedges for serving
- ½ teaspoon honey or agave
- 1 tablespoon tomato paste
- 1 teaspoon chili powder
- ½ teaspoon ground coriander
- ½ teaspoon ground cumin
- ⅛ teaspoon cayenne
- Kosher salt
- 1 medium cauliflower, cored and cut into small florets
- 8 small tortillas, warmed
- Spicy Taco Slaw (see right)
- Chopped fresh cilantro, for topping

1. Heat the air fryer to 380°F. In a large bowl, whisk together the oil, lime juice and honey. Whisk in the tomato paste, chili powder, coriander, cumin, cayenne and ½ teaspoon salt. Add the cauliflower and toss to coat.

2. Transfer half of the cauliflower to the air-fryer basket and air-fry, shaking the basket halfway through, until golden brown, 8 minutes. Transfer the cauliflower to a platter or bowl. Repeat with the remaining cauliflower.

3. Spoon the cauliflower into the tortillas and top with the slaw. Serve with lime wedges and cilantro.

—

PER SERVING *About 360 calories, 16.5 g fat (3.5 g saturated fat), 10 g protein, 1,165 mg sodium, 46 g carbohydrates, 7 g fiber*

Spicy Taco Slaw

In a large bowl, whisk together 2 tablespoons fresh **lime juice**, 1 tablespoon **mayonnaise** and ½ teaspoon **kosher salt**. Add ¼ small head **purple cabbage** (cored and very thinly sliced) and toss to coat, adding more mayonnaise if desired. Toss with 1 small **red pepper** (quartered and thinly sliced) and 1 small **jalapeño** (thinly sliced). Fold in ¼ cup fresh **cilantro** (roughly chopped) just before serving.

Butternut Squash Soup

This hearty bowl of comfort starts in the air fryer, roasting butternut squash, carrots and aromatics until their sugars caramelize. A blender takes you to the finish line, turning it all into a silky-smooth soup.

ACTIVE TIME 20 minutes   TOTAL TIME 45 minutes   SERVES 4

2 ½   pounds butternut squash, peeled and cut into 1-inch pieces

2   medium carrots, cut into 1-inch pieces

1   large onion, cut into ½-inch-thick wedges

4   cloves garlic, 2 whole and 2 thinly sliced

1   red Fresno chile, halved and seeded

4   sprigs thyme

¼   cup olive oil, divided

Kosher salt

2   tablespoons pepitas

¼   teaspoon smoked paprika

Sour cream, for topping

Crusty bread, for serving (optional)

1. Heat the air fryer to 400°F. In a large bowl, toss the squash, carrots, onion, whole garlic, chile, thyme, 2 tablespoons oil and ¾ teaspoon salt. Working in batches if needed, transfer the vegetables to the air-fryer basket and air-fry, shaking the basket occasionally, until tender, 30 minutes. Discard the thyme sprigs.

2. Meanwhile, in a small bowl, toss the sliced garlic with the remaining 2 tablespoons oil. Microwave on High for 30 seconds, then stir and microwave in 30-second increments until the garlic begins to lightly brown around the edges. Add the pepitas, paprika and a pinch of salt and microwave 30 seconds more.

3. Transfer all but ½ cup squash to a blender, add 1 cup water and puree, gradually adding an additional 3 cups water, until smooth. Reheat if necessary and top with sour cream, reserved squash pieces and spiced pepitas. Serve with crusty bread if desired.

—

PER SERVING *About 280 calories, 15.5 g fat (2.5 g saturated fat), 5 g protein, 425 mg sodium, 36 g carbohydrates, 7 g fiber*

love your leftovers

Freeze the leftover soup (without the cream and pepitas) in an airtight container for up to 3 months. To enjoy, thaw the frozen soup overnight in the refrigerator, then warm in the microwave and top as desired.

Pesto-Stuffed Chicken

Stuff each piece of chicken with a cheesy, herby pesto mixture, then wrap with prosciutto. It's a fancy-feeling meal that's fast and easy enough to pull off on a busy weeknight.

ACTIVE TIME 20 minutes   TOTAL TIME 25 minutes   SERVES 4

4   6-ounce boneless, skinless chicken breasts

4   tablespoons pesto

4   tablespoons goat cheese

1 ½   tablespoons olive oil, divided

Kosher salt and pepper

4 to 8 thin slices prosciutto

¼   cup small basil leaves

12   ounces green beans, trimmed

2   large cloves garlic, thinly sliced

1   pint grape or cherry tomatoes, halved

1   scallion, thinly sliced

1. Heat the air fryer to 375°F. Insert a knife into the thickest part of each chicken breast and move the knife back and forth to create a 2 ½-inch pocket that is as wide as possible without going through the chicken.

2. Using a spoon, divide the pesto and goat cheese among the pockets. Rub the chicken with ½ tablespoon oil, then season with salt and pepper.

3. Lay a prosciutto slice on a cutting board and place a few small basil leaves in the center. Place a chicken breast on top of the basil leaves and wrap the prosciutto around the chicken. (You may need to use 2 slices of prosciutto to cover the chicken.) Repeat this process with the remaining slices of prosciutto, basil and chicken breasts. Place the prosciutto-wrapped chicken seam side down in the air-fryer basket. Air-fry 6 minutes.

4. In a medium bowl, toss the green beans and garlic with the remaining tablespoon oil and ¼ teaspoon each salt and pepper. Move the chicken to one side of the basket and place the green beans on the other side. Continue air-frying until the chicken is cooked through (165°F) and the green beans are just tender and slightly charred, 4 to 6 minutes more.

5. Meanwhile, in the same medium bowl, toss the tomatoes and scallion. Spoon on top of the green beans and serve with the chicken.

—

PER SERVING *About 380 calories, 19.5 g fat (5 g saturated fat), 43 g protein, 930 mg sodium, 7 g carbohydrates, 2 g fiber*

TEST KITCHEN TIP
Sub in a different marinade and consider this timing as your guide.

Italian-Marinated Chicken with Mixed Greens

The secret to the juiciest-ever chicken? A supercharged marinade that will become your go-to. Acidic vinegars tenderize the meat, and fresh herbs, sweeteners and a DIY Italian seasoning amp up the flavor of a basic chicken breast.

ACTIVE TIME 25 minutes   TOTAL TIME 45 minutes, plus marinating   SERVES 4

- 3 tablespoons white wine vinegar
- 2 tablespoons red wine vinegar
- 2 cloves garlic
- 2 teaspoons Dijon mustard
- 1 teaspoon honey
- 6 basil leaves
- 1/2 tablespoon fresh thyme
- Kosher salt and pepper
- 2/3 cup olive oil
- 1/2 teaspoon red pepper flakes
- 1/4 teaspoon dried oregano
- 4 6-ounce boneless, skinless chicken breasts
- 2 yellow or orange peppers, thinly sliced
- 1/2 small red onion, thinly sliced
- 12 cups (about 6 ounces) mixed salad greens, torn into bite-size pieces
- 1 ounce Parmesan cheese, shaved

1. In a blender, puree the vinegars, garlic, mustard, honey, basil, thyme and 1/2 teaspoon each salt and pepper until smooth. Add the oil and blend on low until just incorporated but not emulsified, about 10 seconds. Stir in the red pepper flakes and oregano.

2. In a small baking dish, coat the chicken with 1/3 cup of the marinade and marinate at least 10 minutes at room temperature or up to overnight in the refrigerator.

3. Meanwhile, transfer the remaining 3 tablespoons marinade to a large bowl. Add the peppers and onion and toss to coat.

4. When ready to cook, heat the air fryer to 400°F. Working in batches if needed, add the chicken to the air-fryer basket, spacing them apart so they're not touching, and air-fry 4 minutes. Using tongs, flip and air-fry until the chicken is golden brown and cooked through (165°F), 8 to 9 minutes more. Transfer the chicken to a cutting board and let rest 5 minutes before slicing.

5. Add the mixed salad greens to the bowl with the peppers and onion and toss to coat. Top with the cheese and serve with the chicken.
—

PER SERVING *About 425 calories, 24.5 g fat (5 g saturated fat), 39 g protein, 525 mg sodium, 14 g carbohydrates, 3 g fiber*

Mediterranean Chicken Bowls

Loosely inspired by souvlaki, this chicken gets a flavor boost from a mix of dried oregano and sumac, plus these couscous bowls are topped with all the deliciousness of dill and feta. Serve the bowls for dinner or prep and stash them in the fridge for easy lunches. You can enjoy hot or cold.

ACTIVE TIME 15 minutes   TOTAL TIME 30 minutes   SERVES 2 to 4

1 **pound boneless, skinless chicken breasts, cut into 1½-inch pieces**

1 **tablespoon olive oil**

1 **teaspoon dried oregano**

1 **teaspoon ground sumac**

Kosher salt and pepper

1 **pint grape or cherry tomatoes**

1 **medium onion, roughly chopped**

1 **cup couscous**

1 **teaspoon grated lemon zest plus 1 tablespoon fresh lemon juice, plus lemon wedges for serving**

¼ **cup fresh dill, chopped, divided**

Crumbled feta, for topping

1. In a large bowl, toss the chicken with the oil, then with the oregano, sumac and ½ teaspoon each salt and pepper. Add the tomatoes and onion and toss to combine.

2. Heat the air fryer to 400°F. Working in batches if needed, arrange the chicken and vegetables in an even layer in the air-fryer basket and air-fry, shaking the basket occasionally, until the chicken is golden brown and cooked through (165°F), 15 to 20 minutes.

3. Meanwhile, in a medium bowl, toss the couscous with the lemon zest and prepare per the package directions. Fluff the cooked couscous with a fork and fold in the lemon juice and 2 tablespoons dill.

4. Serve the chicken and vegetables over the couscous, spooning any juices over the top. Sprinkle the bowls with the remaining 2 tablespoons dill and feta and serve with lemon wedges.
—

PER SERVING *About 475 calories, 9.5 g fat (1.5 g saturated fat), 43 g protein, 425 mg sodium, 53 g carbohydrates, 5 g fiber*

Garlicky Wings and Shishito Peppers

This essential air-fryer appetizer works as a crowd-pleasing dinner when you add charred shishito peppers to the equation. Be sure to pat the wings dry before cooking in the air fryer for the crispiest (read: tastiest) results.

ACTIVE TIME 20 minutes   TOTAL TIME 25 minutes, plus marinating   SERVES 4

3 tablespoons fish sauce, divided

2 tablespoons fresh lime juice, divided

1 tablespoon plus 1 teaspoon packed brown sugar, divided

4 cloves garlic, 2 pressed and 2 thinly sliced

2 pounds chicken wings

8 ounces shishito peppers

2 tablespoons plus 2 teaspoons canola oil, divided

Kosher salt

1 small red chile, thinly sliced

Chopped fresh cilantro and torn fresh basil, for topping

1. In a large bowl, whisk together 2 tablespoons fish sauce, 1 tablespoon lime juice and 1 tablespoon brown sugar to dissolve, then stir in the pressed garlic, add the wings and toss. Refrigerate the wings to marinate for at least 1 hour or up to 3 hours.

2. Heat the air fryer to 400°F. Transfer the wings to the air-fryer basket, discarding the marinade. Air-fry 8 minutes.

3. In a medium bowl, toss the shishito peppers with 2 teaspoons oil and ¼ teaspoon salt. Using tongs, flip the wings in the basket, scatter the peppers around the wings and continue air-frying until the wings are cooked through and the peppers are browned in spots, 7 minutes more. Transfer the wings and peppers to a platter.

4. Remove the air-fryer insert from the basket, add the remaining 2 tablespoons oil to the air-fryer basket and heat the air fryer to 300°F. (If you're using a toaster-oven-style air fryer, use a small baking sheet instead.) Add the sliced garlic and air-fry for 4 minutes. Add the chile and air-fry until the garlic is golden brown and crisp, 4 minutes more. Transfer the garlic-chile mixture to a medium bowl and stir in the remaining tablespoon each of lime juice, fish sauce and brown sugar. Spoon the sauce over the wings and peppers and sprinkle with herbs.

—

PER SERVING *About 390 calories, 27.5 g fat (6 g saturated fat), 28 g protein, 820 mg sodium, 8 g carbohydrates, 2 g fiber*

TEST KITCHEN TIP
Since the goal is to get tomatoes bursting — instead of crispy — you don't need to stress about leaving extra space for air to circulate.

Salmon Flatbreads

Something magical happens when you roast bite-size tomatoes until they burst. They become a tad saucy, and when tossed with a quick scallion-caper vinaigrette, they add tangy, briny flavor to many dishes. Exhibit A.

ACTIVE TIME 15 minutes TOTAL TIME 15 minutes SERVES 4

1 tablespoon red wine vinegar

2 tablespoons olive oil, divided

1 tablespoon capers, chopped

2 scallions, 1 finely chopped and 1 thinly sliced

Kosher salt and pepper

1 pint grape tomatoes

1 pound skinless salmon fillet, cut into 1-inch pieces

1 tablespoon fresh flat-leaf parsley, chopped

1/2 cup labneh or Greek yogurt, for serving

4 pieces naan or flatbread, warmed

2 cups baby arugula or kale

Crumbled feta, for topping

1. In a small bowl, combine the vinegar, 1 tablespoon oil, capers, chopped scallions and 1/4 teaspoon pepper; set aside.

2. Heat the air fryer to 400°F. In a medium bowl, toss the tomatoes with the remaining 1 tablespoon oil and 1/4 teaspoon each salt and pepper. Season the salmon with 1/4 teaspoon each salt and pepper.

3. Working in batches if needed, place the salmon in a single layer on one side of the air-fryer basket and add the tomatoes to the remaining space (piling them up is great). Air-fry until the salmon is barely opaque throughout (145°F) and the tomatoes are beginning to burst, 6 minutes.

4. Transfer the tomatoes to the small bowl with the scallion-caper vinaigrette and toss to combine. Add the parsley and toss well.

5. Spread the labneh on the naan and top with the salmon and baby arugula. Spoon the tomato mixture on top. Sprinkle with the sliced scallions and crumbled feta.

—

PER SERVING *About 485 calories, 25 g fat (9 g saturated fat), 41 g protein, 750 mg sodium, 30 g carbohydrates, 10 g fiber*

TEST KITCHEN TIP
Gochujang delivers heat, but it can vary in spice level depending on the brand. Taste a tiny bit beforehand and adjust the amount based on your tolerance for heat.

Spicy Shrimp Lettuce Wraps

Large plump shrimp coated in a sweet and spicy sauce are hard to resist. Plus, this customizable family-style dinner allows everyone to choose their own toppings while assembling — so no complaints here! Want to dial up the heat? Make a double batch of the fiery marinade, then set some aside for serving so people can drizzle it.

ACTIVE TIME 20 minutes   TOTAL TIME 20 minutes   SERVES 6

2 **tablespoons fresh lemon juice**

1½ **to 2 tablespoons gochujang**

1 **tablespoon olive oil**

2 **teaspoons honey**

1 **clove garlic, grated**

2 **teaspoons grated peeled fresh ginger**

1½ **pounds peeled and deveined large shrimp**

1 **head Boston lettuce, leaves separated**

2 **Persian cucumbers, sliced**

1 **bunch small radishes, sliced**

  Fresh mint and basil, for topping

1. Heat the air fryer to 380°F. In a large bowl, whisk together the lemon juice, gochujang, oil and honey, then stir in the garlic and ginger. Add the shrimp and toss to coat.

2. Working in batches if needed, arrange the shrimp in a single layer in the air-fryer basket and air-fry until just opaque throughout, 3 to 4 minutes.

3. Serve the shrimp with the lettuce, cucumbers, radishes, mint and basil for assembly.

—

PER SERVING *About 230 calories, 4.5 g fat (0.5 g saturated fat), 36 g protein, 705 mg sodium, 13 g carbohydrates, 1 g fiber*

Fish and "Chips"

Consider this five-ingredient dinner your excuse to pick up a few extra bags of salt-and-vinegar chips from the grocery store. Crushed, they work as a crisp coating for fish that can sub in for breadcrumbs on any given fish Friday.

ACTIVE TIME 10 minutes TOTAL TIME 20 minutes SERVES 4

2 large egg whites

2 5-ounce packages salt-and-vinegar potato chips

1½ pounds cod or hake fillets

1 tablespoon olive oil, plus more for brushing

1 16-ounce package frozen peas, thawed

1 teaspoon grated lemon zest plus 2 tablespoons fresh lemon juice

Kosher salt and pepper

1. Heat the air fryer to 400°F. In a shallow bowl, beat the egg whites with 1 tablespoon water.

2. Crush the potato chips (you should have about 4 cups) and place in a second shallow bowl.

3. Cut the fish fillets into 3-inch pieces. Dip each piece in the egg whites, letting the excess drip off, then coat in the crushed chips, pressing gently to help the chip pieces adhere. Working in batches if needed, brush the air-fryer basket with oil, add the fish, spacing them apart so they're not touching, and air-fry until golden brown and opaque throughout (145°F), 10 minutes.

4. Meanwhile, in a medium bowl, microwave the peas on Medium for 2 minutes. Toss with the lemon zest and juice, 1 tablespoon oil and ½ teaspoon each salt and pepper. Mash the peas and serve them with the fish.

—

PER SERVING *About 660 calories, 30 g fat (4.5 g saturated fat), 40 g protein, 915 mg sodium, 54 g carbohydrates, 8 g fiber*

TEST KITCHEN TIP
If you prefer salmon fillets without the skin, all good! We tested and this cooking method works beautifully with those as well.

Salmon and Swiss Chard

Instead of sautéing this sturdy green, throw it in the air fryer before cooking up flaky salmon fillets. The result? Chard that is slightly charred, perfectly tender and infused with aromatic flavors.

ACTIVE TIME 25 minutes TOTAL TIME 25 minutes SERVES 4

1 medium red onion, sliced ½ inch thick

1½ tablespoons olive oil, divided

Kosher salt and pepper

1 large bunch red Swiss chard, thick stems discarded, leaves chopped

2 cloves garlic, sliced

4 5-ounce skin-on salmon fillets

Chili oil, for topping (optional)

1. Heat the air fryer to 385°F. In a medium bowl, toss the onion with ½ tablespoon oil and a pinch each of salt and pepper; add to the air-fryer basket and air-fry 5 minutes.

2. Add the Swiss chard to the basket with the onion and toss with the garlic, remaining 1 tablespoon oil and ¼ teaspoon each salt and pepper and air-fry until the chard and onion are just tender, about 5 minutes more. Transfer the greens to plates.

3. Heat the air fryer to 400°F. Season the salmon with ½ teaspoon each salt and pepper, add to the basket skin side up and air-fry until the skin is crispy and the salmon is opaque throughout (145°F), 8 to 10 minutes. Serve with the chard and drizzle with chili oil if desired.

—

PER SERVING *About 245 calories, 10.5 g fat (2 g saturated fat), 30 g protein, 640 mg sodium, 7 g carbohydrates, 2 g fiber*

TEST KITCHEN TIP

Use your air fryer to warm the tortillas! Heat to 380°F, then air-fry 2 minutes. Wrap them in aluminum foil or a kitchen towel to keep warm while you prepare the rest of the recipe.

Steak Fajitas

Enjoy sizzling restaurant-quality fajitas at home — no grill or specialty equipment required. Choose between skirt and hanger steak, based on what's available (or on sale). To ensure that the meat won't dry out, cut it into pieces that are just small enough to fit inside your air-fryer basket. Then thinly slice the meat after it is cooked and has a chance to rest for a few minutes.

ACTIVE TIME 15 minutes　TOTAL TIME 35 minutes　SERVES 2 to 4

- 2 large red or yellow peppers, quartered lengthwise, then sliced crosswise ¼ inch thick
- 1 large red onion, sliced ¼ inch thick
- 2 teaspoons grated lime zest plus 2 tablespoons fresh lime juice, plus lime wedges for serving
- ¼ teaspoon ground cumin
- 1 tablespoon plus 2 teaspoons canola oil, divided
- ½ teaspoon granulated garlic, divided
- Kosher salt and pepper
- 12 ounces skirt steak, cut crosswise into 4-inch pieces, or hanger steak, halved
- 1 teaspoon ancho chile powder
- ¼ cup fresh cilantro, chopped, plus more for topping
- 8 6-inch flour tortillas, warmed
- Sour cream, for topping

1. In a large bowl, toss the peppers and onion with the lime zest and juice, cumin, 1 tablespoon oil, ¼ teaspoon garlic, ½ teaspoon salt and ¼ teaspoon pepper. Heat the air fryer to 400°F. Working in batches if needed, add the peppers and onion to the air-fryer basket; air-fry, shaking occasionally, 10 minutes.

2. Meanwhile, rub the steak with the remaining 2 teaspoons oil, then season with the ancho chile powder, remaining ¼ teaspoon garlic and ½ teaspoon each salt and pepper. Push the vegetables to one side of the basket and add the steak to the other side. Air-fry the steak to desired doneness, flipping once halfway through, 10 minutes for medium-rare (135°).

3. Transfer the steak to a cutting board and let rest for at least 5 minutes before slicing. Toss the cooked vegetables with the cilantro. Fill the tortillas with the steak, peppers and onions, then top with sour cream. Sprinkle with cilantro and serve with lime wedges.
—

PER SERVING *About 615 calories, 28 g fat (8 g saturated fat), 35 g protein, 1,500 mg sodium, 57 g carbohydrates, 6 g fiber*

Gingery Pork Burgers

Bring the backyard BBQ inside! Your air fryer can work some magic as a stand-in grill, providing you with a far less smoky — yet equally flavorful — alternative when cooking burgers indoors. Here, we're using ground pork, but you can also cook up any beef or turkey burgers in the air fryer.

ACTIVE TIME 25 minutes TOTAL TIME 25 minutes SERVES 4

1 large egg

2 teaspoons grated lime zest plus 2 tablespoons fresh lime juice

1½ tablespoons honey

1 teaspoon fish sauce

Kosher salt

½ cup panko

3 cloves garlic, grated

2 scallions, finely chopped

1 tablespoon grated peeled fresh ginger

1 small jalapeño, halved, seeded and finely chopped

1 pound ground pork

¼ cup fresh cilantro, chopped

4 hamburger buns, split, toasted if desired

Carrot and Cucumber Salad (see right)

1. Make the burgers: In a large bowl, whisk together the egg, lime zest and juice, honey, fish sauce and ½ teaspoon salt; stir in the panko and let sit 1 minute. Stir in the garlic, scallions, ginger and jalapeño. Add the pork and cilantro and mix to combine (being careful to avoid overmixing). Shape the mixture into four 5-inch burgers.

2. Heat the air fryer to 400°F. Working in batches if needed, add the burgers to the air-fryer basket in a single layer and air-fry 9 minutes. Using tongs or a spatula, flip the burgers and air-fry until browned and cooked through (160°F), 5 minutes more.

3. Place the burgers on the bottom buns, top with the salad and sandwich with the bun tops.

—

PER SERVING *About 500 calories, 20 g fat (7 g saturated fat), 30 g protein, 805 mg sodium, 49 g carbohydrates, 3 g fiber*

Carrot and Cucumber Salad

In a large bowl, whisk together 2 tablespoons **rice vinegar**, 1 tablespoon fresh **lime juice**, ½ teaspoon **fish sauce**, ½ teaspoon **sugar** and 1 small clove **garlic** (grated). Add 2 medium or large **carrots** (sliced into thin ribbons), 2 small **Persian cucumbers** (sliced into thin ribbons), 4 **radishes** (thinly sliced), 2 **scallions** (thinly sliced) and 2 tablespoons **mint leaves** (torn) and toss to combine.

Meatball Subs

Whip up batches of tender, evenly browned meatballs — without the mess of pan-frying. Made with a combination of sweet Italian sausage and ground beef, these meatballs are juicy and super flavorful. We whisked a splash of balsamic vinegar in with the eggs for a little extra punch. Perfect for piling atop a bed of spaghetti or stuffing into hero rolls.

ACTIVE TIME 20 minutes   TOTAL TIME 30 minutes   SERVES 4

2 **large eggs**

2 **teaspoons balsamic vinegar**

Kosher salt and pepper

1/3 **cup panko**

4 **large cloves garlic, 2 grated and 2 chopped**

1/4 **cup grated Parmesan cheese, plus more for topping**

1/2 **cup fresh flat-leaf parsley, chopped**

8 **ounces sweet Italian sausage, casings removed**

8 **ounces ground beef**

1 **pound cherry tomatoes**

1 **red chile, sliced**

1 **tablespoon olive oil**

6 **tablespoons ricotta cheese**

4 **small hero rolls, split and toasted**

Chopped fresh basil, for topping (optional)

1. In a large bowl, whisk together the eggs, vinegar and 1/2 teaspoon each salt and pepper. Stir in the panko and let sit 1 minute. Stir in the grated garlic and Parmesan, then the parsley. Add the sausage and ground beef and gently mix to combine (being careful to avoid overmixing). Shape the meat mixture into 20 balls (about 1 1/2 inches each).

2. Heat the air fryer to 400°F. Working in batches if needed, arrange the meatballs in a single layer in the air-fryer basket (they can touch but should not be stacked) and air-fry 5 minutes.

3. In a medium bowl, toss the tomatoes, chile and chopped garlic with the oil and 1/4 teaspoon each salt and pepper. Once all the meatballs are air-fried, return them to the basket (stacking is OK at this point). Scatter the tomatoes over the meatballs and continue air-frying until the meatballs are cooked through (160°F), 5 to 6 minutes more.

4. Spread the ricotta on the toasted rolls. Top with the meatballs, tomatoes, more Parmesan and basil if desired.

—

PER SERVING *About 600 calories, 31 g fat (11 g saturated fat), 26 g protein, 1,065 mg sodium, 51 g carbohydrates, 5 g fiber*

meal prep magic

Make a few extra meatball batches to stash in the freezer, so you always have a back-pocket meal ready to go. Freeze cooked meatballs on a baking sheet until solid, then transfer to freezer bags or freezer-safe containers (labeled with the date). Reheat in the air fryer and toss with cooked spaghetti and jarred marinara.

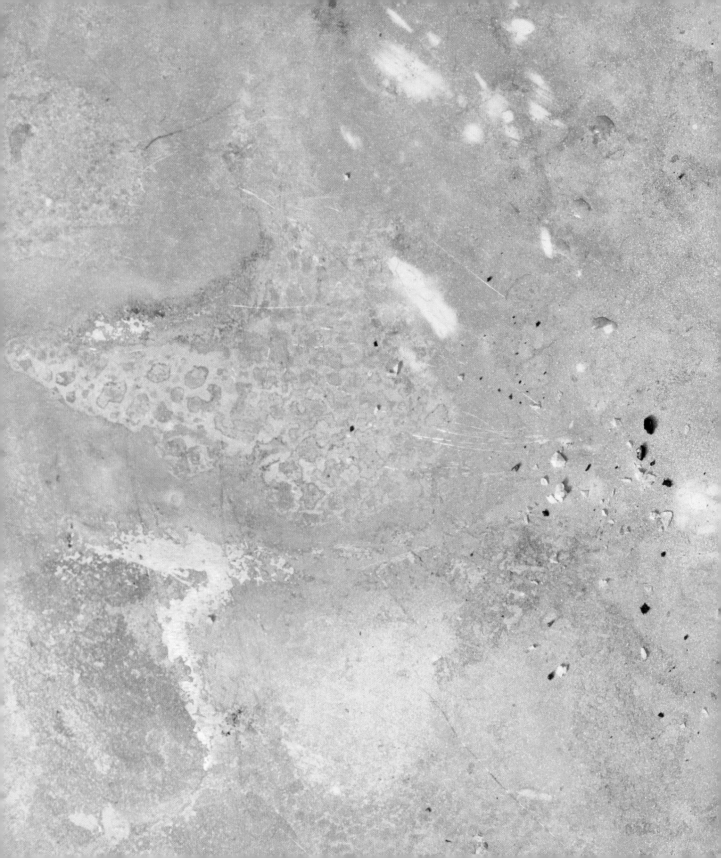

chapter six

Desserts

The air fryer can help you make sweets —
everything from freshly "fried" donuts to quickly
baked carrot breads and small-batch
sweets — without heating up your entire kitchen.

RECIPES

Quick-Fix Donuts

There is something almost magical about a fresh-from-the-deep-fryer donut. Pillowy, warm and coated with a light dusting of sugar, this treat just can't be beat. This shortcut version — yielding donuts and donut holes — comes close and takes far less work. A can of store-bought biscuit dough saves time and avoids the hassle of making a yeasted dough from scratch.

ACTIVE TIME 10 minutes   **TOTAL TIME** 30 minutes   **MAKES** 8 donuts and 8 donut holes

FOR THE DONUTS

- 1 16-ounce can refrigerated biscuit dough
- Melted butter, for brushing

FOR THE RASPBERRY SUGAR

- ½ cup freeze-dried raspberries
- ¼ cup sugar

FOR THE CHAI SUGAR

- ¼ cup sugar
- ½ to ¼ teaspoon ground cardamom
- ¼ teaspoon ground cinnamon
- ¼ teaspoon ground ginger
- ⅛ teaspoon allspice
- Pinch ground cloves

1. Make the donuts: Heat the air fryer to 350°F. Separate the biscuits onto a parchment-lined baking sheet. Use a 1 ¼-inch round cutter to cut out a hole in the center of each biscuit. Reserve the holes.

2. Brush the air-fryer basket with melted butter. Working in batches if needed, arrange the donuts in the basket, spacing them apart so they're not touching. Air-fry, flipping the donuts halfway through, until golden brown, 6 to 8 minutes. Transfer to a wire rack.

3. Arrange the donut holes in the basket and air-fry, flipping them halfway through, until golden brown, 4 to 5 minutes.

4. While the donuts are cooking, prepare the sugars. To make the raspberry sugar: In a mini food processor, pulse the freeze-dried raspberries with the sugar until finely ground. Use a sieve to sift out any seeds. To make the chai sugar: In a small bowl, using your fingers, combine the sugar, cardamom, cinnamon, ginger, allspice and cloves until the mixture is uniform.

5. After removing the donuts and donut holes from the air fryer, immediately brush them with melted butter and toss them in your choice of sugar mixture.

—

PER SERVING (1 DONUT AND 1 DONUT HOLE) *About 235 calories, 11 g fat (5 g saturated fat), 4 g protein, 640 mg sodium, 31 g carbohydrates, 1 g fiber*

Red Velvet Cookies

Whip up a big batch of cookie dough to "bake" off in batches or store in the freezer to air-fry at a moment's notice.

ACTIVE TIME 20 minutes   **TOTAL TIME** 35 minutes   **MAKES** 36

2 **cups all-purpose flour**

1/2 **cup Dutch-process cocoa powder**

1 **teaspoon baking soda**

1 **teaspoon kosher salt**

1 **cup (2 sticks) unsalted butter, at room temperature**

3/4 **cup packed light brown sugar**

1/2 **cup granulated sugar**

1 **large egg, at room temperature**

2 **teaspoons pure vanilla extract**

1 **teaspoon red gel food coloring**

1 **12-ounce package semisweet chocolate chips**

1. In a large bowl, whisk together the flour, cocoa, baking soda and salt.

2. Using an electric stand mixer on medium speed, beat together the butter and sugars until light and fluffy, 2 to 3 minutes. Scrape down the bowl, reduce the speed to low, then add the egg, vanilla and food coloring. Once the dough is beginning to incorporate, increase the speed to medium and mix until fully combined.

3. Reduce the mixer speed to low and gradually add the flour mixture; mix until just combined. Fold in the chocolate chips.

4. Line the air fryer basket with a piece of parchment paper, leaving enough space along the edges to allow for air circulation. Heat the air fryer to 300°F.

5. Scoop 2 tablespoons of dough per cookie. Working in batches if needed, place the cookies 2 inches apart in the parchment-lined air-fryer basket. Air-fry until the cookies are set and the tops are slightly cracked, 14 to 15 minutes. Remove the cookies from the air fryer immediately and let set for 5 minutes, then transfer to a wire rack to cool completely.

6. If working in batches, repeat step 5 with the remaining dough. Alternatively, freeze the remaining dough: Add scoops of dough to a parchment-lined baking sheet and freeze 30 minutes, then transfer to a freezer-safe airtight container or resealable plastic bag, labeled with the date, and store in the freezer for up to 3 months. Air-fry from frozen until the cookies are set and the tops are slightly cracked, 16 to 18 minutes.

—

PER SERVING *About 65 calories, 2 g fat (1 g saturated fat), 1 g protein, 50 mg sodium, 12 g carbohydrates, 0 g fiber*

Peanut Butter Molten Chocolate Cakes

We made two batches of this recipe to taste side by side — one baked in a conventional oven and another prepared in the air fryer — and found a clear winner. The air-fried version was slightly chewy with crisp edges and a melty, nutty center. Yum! Adding baking powder to the batter helps to give these cakes some height (read: it makes them more visually stunning).

ACTIVE TIME 25 minutes   **TOTAL TIME** 45 minutes   **MAKES** 6

¾ cup (1 ½ sticks) **unsalted butter**, cut into pieces, plus more for greasing

⅓ cup **granulated sugar**, plus more for dusting

6 ounces **semisweet chocolate chips**

3 **large eggs**, at room temperature

3 **large egg yolks**, at room temperature

1 teaspoon **pure vanilla extract**

¼ teaspoon **kosher salt**

⅓ cup **all-purpose flour**

1 tablespoon **unsweetened cocoa powder**, plus more for dusting (optional)

½ teaspoon **baking powder**

⅓ cup **creamy peanut butter** (do not use the natural type)

3 tablespoons **confectioners' sugar**

1. In a medium saucepan, bring 1 inch of water to a simmer. Butter six 6-ounce ramekins and dust them with granulated sugar.

2. In a heatproof bowl, combine the chocolate chips and butter and place the bowl over but not in the simmering water. Gently melt the chocolate and butter, stirring occasionally, until smooth. Remove the bowl from the heat and let cool slightly.

3. Meanwhile, in a medium bowl, whisk together the granulated sugar, eggs, egg yolks, vanilla and salt until well combined. In a small bowl, whisk together the flour, cocoa powder and baking powder.

4. Add the egg mixture to the cooled chocolate mixture and whisk to combine. Add the flour mixture and gently whisk together until the batter is smooth. Divide half of the batter among the prepared ramekins.

5. Heat the air fryer to 370°F. In a small bowl, stir together the peanut butter and confectioners' sugar until combined. Scoop 1 tablespoon of the peanut butter mixture into each half-filled ramekin. Divide the remaining batter among the ramekins, spooning it over the peanut butter.

6. Working in batches if needed, place the ramekins in the air-fryer basket and air-fry until the cakes have puffed and are set, about 8 minutes. Using a dish towel, carefully remove the ramekins and let them rest for 2 minutes. Loosen the edges of the cakes with a small offset spatula and carefully invert onto plates to serve. Dust with additional cocoa powder if desired.

—

PER SERVING *About 590 calories, 44.5 g fat (23 g saturated fat), 10 g protein, 235 mg sodium, 45 g carbohydrates, 3 g fiber*

TEST KITCHEN TIP
Put your air fryer
to work before you
start baking:
Use the appliance
to toast nuts (350°F
for 4 to 5 minutes).

Jammy Walnut Rugelach

These cookies are more like bite-size pastries. Top flaky, buttery pie crust with spiced sugars, bright jam and walnuts, then roll 'em up for a mini treat.

ACTIVE TIME 35 minutes **TOTAL TIME** 2 hours **MAKES** 24

2/3 cup walnuts

1/4 cup sugar

1/2 teaspoon ground cinnamon

    Pinch ground cloves

2 refrigerated rolled pie crusts or 2 batches Best-Ever Pie Dough (page 29)

    Flour, for rolling

1/2 cup apricot jam, divided

1 large egg

1. In a small bowl, combine the sugar, cinnamon and cloves. Transfer 1 tablespoon of the mixture to a second bowl and set aside. Line a baking sheet with parchment paper.

2. On a lightly floured surface, gently unroll 1 pie crust (if stiff, let it warm up for a few minutes at room temperature). Roll out the dough to a rectangle that is approximately 12 1/2 by 11 inches, sprinkling the top of the dough with flour as needed to prevent sticking.

3. Spread 1/4 cup apricot jam on top of the dough, then sprinkle with half of the spiced sugar and half of the chopped walnuts. Starting from the longer side closest to you, gently roll up the dough into a tight log and transfer to the prepared baking sheet. Repeat steps with the other pie crust. Freeze the logs for 30 minutes.

4. Using a sharp serrated knife, cut each log into 12 1-inch pieces (there should be a total of 24 rugelach). Transfer the rugelach back to the baking sheet and freeze for an additional 15 minutes.

5. Line the air-fryer basket with a piece of parchment paper, leaving enough space along the edges to allow for air circulation. Heat the air fryer to 350°F. In a small bowl, whisk together the egg with a splash of water. Lightly brush the rugelach with the egg wash and sprinkle with the reserved 1 tablespoon spiced sugar.

6. Working in batches if needed, arrange the rugelach 1 inch apart in the parchment-lined basket. Air-fry until the tops are golden brown, 10 to 11 minutes. Using tongs, carefully flip the rugelach and air-fry until the bottoms are golden and the rugelach are cooked through, 9 to 10 minutes more. Transfer to a wire rack to cool completely.

—

PER SERVING *About 115 calories, 6 g fat (2 g saturated fat), 1 g protein, 90 mg sodium, 15 g carbohydrates, 0 g fiber*

Carrot Breads

When we realized that mini loaf pans would fit in the air fryer, we knew it would be the solve for "quick" breads that often take more than an hour to bake in a conventional oven. These get their flavor from shredded carrots, pecans and coconut.

ACTIVE TIME 30 minutes   **TOTAL TIME** 1 hour 5 minutes   **MAKES** 2 mini loaves

Butter, for greasing

½ cup all-purpose flour, plus more for dusting

½ teaspoon baking powder

½ teaspoon baking soda

1 ¼ teaspoons ground cinnamon

¼ teaspoon kosher salt

½ cup packed light brown sugar

2 large eggs

1 teaspoon pure vanilla extract

⅓ cup canola oil

4 medium carrots, peeled and finely grated (about 1 ¼ cups)

½ Granny Smith apple, peeled, cored and coarsely grated (about ½ cup)

¼ cup raisins, chopped

¼ cup shredded sweetened coconut

½ cup pecans, chopped, divided

1 tablespoon sanding sugar (optional)

Salted butter, for topping (optional)

1. Butter two 2-cup mini loaf pans (about 5 ½ by 3 inches) and dust with flour. In a medium bowl, whisk together the flour, baking powder, baking soda, cinnamon and salt.

2. In a large bowl, whisk together the brown sugar, eggs and vanilla until fully incorporated. Whisk in the oil. Fold in the dry ingredients until just combined (avoid overmixing, which will develop the gluten in the flour). Fold in the carrots, apple, raisins, coconut and all but 2 tablespoons of the pecans.

3. Heat the air fryer to 330°F. Divide the batter among the prepared pans (about 1 ⅓ cups in each pan) and top with the sanding sugar (if using). Sprinkle the reserved 2 tablespoons pecans on top, pressing into the batter so they are not sticking out.

4. Working in batches if needed, place the pans in the air-fryer basket and air-fry until deep golden brown and a toothpick inserted in the center comes out with moist crumbs, about 35 minutes. Let the breads cool completely in the pans before serving (they will continue to cook while cooling). Once cool, slice and top with butter if desired.

—

PER SERVING *About 285 calories, 17 g fat (3 g saturated fat), 4 g protein, 235 mg sodium, 32 g carbohydrates, 3 g fiber*

Apples in a Blanket

Crescent roll dough puffs up beautifully in the air fryer. Take a moment to wrap this store-bought dough around apple slices and add a pinch of sugar and spice, and poof — pillowy pieces of happiness coming right up.

ACTIVE TIME 20 minutes **TOTAL TIME** 45 minutes **MAKES** 8

¼ cup sugar

½ teaspoon apple pie spice or cinnamon

1 8-ounce can refrigerated crescent roll dough

3 tablespoons unsalted butter, melted

1 large apple (unpeeled), cored and sliced ¼ inch thick

Oil, for brushing

Salted butter, for serving (optional)

1. In a small bowl, combine the sugar and apple pie spice.

2. Heat the air fryer to 325°F. Separate the dough along the perforations and cut triangles in half lengthwise. Line a baking sheet with parchment paper.

3. Brush the triangles with some of the melted butter and sprinkle them with some of the sugar mixture (reserving some for the next step). Place 2 apple slices at the wide end of one triangle and tightly roll up toward the tip; place on the prepared baking sheet. Repeat with the remaining dough triangles and apple slices.

4. Brush the assembled apple crescents with the remaining melted butter and sprinkle the remaining sugar mixture on top.

5. Brush the air-fryer basket with oil. Working in batches if needed, arrange the apple crescents in the basket, spacing them about 1 inch apart so they're not touching. Air-fry until golden brown, about 8 minutes. Using tongs, flip the apple crescents and air-fry until golden brown on all sides, 2 to 3 minutes more. Transfer to a wire rack to cool slightly before serving.

—

PER SERVING *About 170 calories, 8 g fat (4 g saturated fat), 2 g protein, 215 mg sodium, 24 g carbohydrates, 1 g fiber*

love your leftovers

Store prepared apple pastries in an airtight container for up to 2 days. To enjoy, reheat in the air fryer at 350°F for 4 to 6 minutes.

TEST KITCHEN TIP
Parchment paper helps to prevent dough from falling to the bottom of your air fryer, but it blocks some of the airflow. Adding butter to the piece of parchment works to get your bottoms golden brown.

Strawberry-Thyme Mini Scones

The air fryer gives the outside of the scones a bit of color without drying out the inside, which doesn't always happen in a conventional oven. Avoid overmixing the dough, which often leads to tough and chewy scones. (Not a fan of thyme? We made a batch without it during testing and can vouch that the scones still came out absolutely delightful.)

ACTIVE TIME 15 minutes **TOTAL TIME** 1 hour 35 minutes **MAKES** 8

1 cup all-purpose flour

3 tablespoons sugar, divided

1/2 tablespoon baking powder

1/4 teaspoon kosher salt

3 tablespoons unsalted butter, cut into small pieces, plus softened butter for greasing

1 teaspoon fresh thyme

1/2 cup heavy cream, divided

4 ounces strawberries, quartered

1. In a large bowl, whisk together the flour, 2 1/2 tablespoons sugar, baking powder and salt. Add the butter and cut it in with a pastry blender or your fingers until coarse, irregular crumbs form; toss with the thyme.

2. Add 7 tablespoons heavy cream and mix until just combined and a tiny handful of mixture holds together when squeezed. Fold in the strawberries.

3. Turn the mixture out onto a parchment-lined work surface and press together into a mass. Fold the mixture in half onto itself two or three times, using a piece of parchment as a guide, until the dough comes together. Shape the dough into a 1-inch-thick disk (about 5 inches in diameter). Cut it into 8 wedges.

4. Cut a piece of parchment to the size of the air-fryer basket, brush lightly with softened butter and place in the basket butter side up. Heat the air fryer to 355°F. Working in batches if needed, carefully arrange the scones in the parchment-lined basket, pointed side facing in, and spread as far apart as possible. Brush the tops with remaining 1 tablespoon cream and sprinkle with remaining 1/2 tablespoon sugar. Air-fry until golden brown, 10 to 14 minutes.

5. Immediately transfer the scones to a wire rack to cool slightly before serving.

—

PER SERVING *About 175 calories, 10 g fat (6.5 g saturated fat), 2 g protein, 170 mg sodium, 19 g carbohydrates, 1 g fiber*

TEST KITCHEN TIP

For a fun twist on à la mode, sandwich a scoop of ice cream (about ¼ cup) between 2 hand pies. Try with vanilla bean, coffee or your favorite flavor.

Cranberry-Apple Hand Pies

If your ideal crust-to-filling ratio lands around 2:1, allow us to introduce you to these hand pies — a flaky butter crust surrounds a sweet-tart fruit medley filling. To achieve picture-perfect results, keep your pie dough as cold as possible. Once you've assembled your hand pies, stash them in the fridge or freezer until you're ready to drop them into the air fryer.

ACTIVE TIME 35 minutes **TOTAL TIME** 1 hour 20 minutes **MAKES** 10

3 tablespoons apricot jam

½ teaspoon pure vanilla extract

1 small Gala apple, peeled, cored and cut into ¼-inch pieces

¼ cup cranberries, thawed if frozen

6 tablespoons sugar, divided

½ teaspoon ground cinnamon, divided

Flour, for dusting

2 refrigerated rolled pie crusts or 2 batches Best-Ever Pie Dough (page 29)

1 large egg

1 tablespoon milk

Oil or melted butter, for brushing

1. In a medium bowl, whisk together the jam and vanilla. Add the apple, cranberries, 3 tablespoons sugar and ¼ teaspoon cinnamon and toss to combine.

2. On a lightly floured surface, working with 1 pie crust at a time, gently unroll the dough (if stiff, let it warm up for a few minutes at room temperature). Using a 3-inch round cutter, cut out circles. Reroll the dough and cut out the scraps. (You should end up with about 10 circles per pie crust.) Repeat with the remaining pie crust.

3. Spoon 1 tablespoon of apple filling onto half of the dough circles. In a small bowl, beat the egg with the milk. Brush the borders of the dough with some of the beaten egg. Place the remaining dough circles on top and use a floured fork to firmly crimp the edges together. Place the pies on a parchment-lined baking sheet and freeze for 15 minutes.

4. During the last few minutes of freezing, heat the air fryer to 350°F.

5. In a small bowl, combine the remaining 3 tablespoons sugar and ¼ teaspoon cinnamon. Brush the pies with the beaten egg and sprinkle with the cinnamon sugar. Using a sharp knife, make a small slit on the top of each pie.

6. Brush the air-fryer basket with oil or melted butter. Working in batches if needed, arrange the hand pies in the basket, spacing them 1 inch apart so they're not touching, and air-fry until the tops are golden brown, about 10 minutes. Using tongs, carefully flip the pies. Air-fry until lightly golden brown, 2 to 3 minutes more. Transfer to a wire rack to cool.

—

PER SERVING *About 275 calories, 13 g fat (5 g saturated fat), 2 g protein, 200 mg sodium, 37 g carbohydrates, 1 g fiber*

Blueberry and Blackberry Crumbles

This buttery cinnamon-oat topping works with so many types of fruit, but we especially love it piled on top of freshly burst berries. We popped a few ramekins in the fridge before air-frying to see what would happen but found no discernible difference in the crumb topping. That said, you can make a larger batch of this topping to store in the freezer, so you'll always have a crumble ready to go.

ACTIVE TIME 15 minutes   **TOTAL TIME** 30 minutes   **MAKES** 4

FOR THE TOPPING

- ⅓ cup rolled oats
- ⅓ cup packed light brown sugar
- ⅓ cup all-purpose flour
- ¼ teaspoon kosher salt
- ½ teaspoon ground cinnamon
- 5 tablespoons cold unsalted butter, cut into pieces, plus more for greasing

FOR THE FILLING

- 3 tablespoons granulated sugar
- 2 teaspoons cornstarch
- 1 pint blueberries (about 2 cups)
- 1 6-ounce container blackberries (about 1 cup)
- 1 teaspoon fresh lemon juice

1. Make the topping: In a medium bowl, combine the oats, brown sugar, flour, salt and cinnamon. Using a fork or your fingers, rub the butter into the mixture until it is crumbly and resembles wet sand.

2. Heat the air fryer to 340°F. Butter four 6-ounce ramekins.

3. Make the filling: In a medium bowl, whisk together the granulated sugar and cornstarch. Add the berries and lemon juice and toss to combine. Divide among the ramekins.

4. Crumble the oat mixture on top of the fruit. Working in batches if needed, place the ramekins in the air-fryer basket and air-fry until the topping is golden brown and the fruit mixture is bubbling throughout, 13 to 15 minutes. Let rest for at least 5 minutes before serving.

—

PER SERVING *About 375 calories, 17 g fat (10 g saturated fat), 3 g protein, 130 mg sodium, 56 g carbohydrates, 5 g fiber*

Index

Credits

PHOTOGRAPHY
Mike Garten 4, 8–9, 18–19, 25, 32, 36–37, 42, 44, 48,
50, 54, 56, 58,68–69, 76, 78, 80, 82, 86, 88, 90,
94–95, 96, 100, 102, 104, 105, 106, 110, 114, 116, 120–121,
122, 124, 126, 128, 131, 132, 133, 136, 138, 140, 142, 144,
146, 148, 150, 152–153, 156, 158, 172–176

Lucy Schaeffer 26

Danielle Daly 28, 108

Courtesy of companies 12, 13

FOOD STYLING
Christine Albano, Simon Andrews,
Sue Li, Sherry Rujikarn

PROP STYLING
Lis Engelhart, Cate Geiger Kalus, Emily Luppino,
Christina Lane, Alex Mata, Pam Morris

VISUAL DIRECTORS
Bruce Perez, Cinzia Reale-Castello

RECIPE DEVELOPMENT
Joy Cho, Kristina Kurek, Tina Martinez,
Kate Merker, Nicole Papantoniou

EDITORS
Trish Clasen Marsanico, Nicole Fisher,
Kate Merker

COVER AND BOOK DESIGN
Erynn Hassinger